What Color Is Your Parachute?
for teens

RICHARD N. BOLLES PRESENTS

WHAT COLOR IS YOUR
PARACHUTE?
for teens

Discover Yourself, Design Your Future,
and Plan for Your Dream Job

Third Edition

BY CAROL CHRISTEN

TEN SPEED PRESS
Berkeley

This edition is dedicated to my daughter and husband. Thank you both for putting up with me. Both of these beloved people have made great efforts to put together lives they love financed by work they enjoy. If they can do it, dear reader, so can you.

Copyright © 2006, 2010, 2015 by Carol Christen and Richard Nelson Bolles

Published in the United States by Ten Speed Press, an imprint of the Crown Publishing Group, a division of Penguin Random House LLC, New York.

www.crownpublishing.com
www.tenspeed.com

Ten Speed Press and the Ten Speed Press colophon are registered trademarks of Penguin Random House LLC.

Previous editions of this book were published by Ten Speed Press in 2006 and 2010.

Images on page 25 used by permission of DreamMaker Publishing, Inc.

Library of Congress Cataloging-in-Publication Data

Christen, Carol.

What color is your parachute? for teens : discover yourself, design your future, and plan for your dream job / Carol Christen and Richard N. Bolles. — Third edition.

pages cm

Includes index.

1. Teenagers—Vocational guidance. 2. Job hunting. I. Bolles, Richard Nelson. II. Title.

HF5381.B63513 2016

650.140835—dc23

2014046344

Trade Paperback ISBN: 978-1-60774-577-8
eBook ISBN: 978-1-60774-578-5

Design by Margaux Keres

Cover photograph copyright © Peter Cade/Getty Images

Printed in the United States of America

10 9 8 7 6

Third Edition

CONTENTS

ACKNOWLEDGMENTS

This book grew from a conversation over tea with the late Phil Wood, friend and founder of Ten Speed Press, and his wife, Winifred Wood. Phil's call in January 2004 to ask of my interest in writing a *Parachute* book for youth allowed me to distill my Parachute experiences with young adults into a DIY book on career choice and job searching. The English-language edition is found on every continent. Thanks to Captain Tim Forderer (www.dwylmentors.blogspot.com), this book is even in remote archipelagoes such as the Komodo Islands. It has been translated into Dutch, German, and Vietnamese.

Every writer should have an editor like Lisa Westmoreland. She tempers my more radical starts, plays excellent manuscript Frisbee, and is just plain fun. Under her guidance, this has become the book I envisioned. Melissa Stein is a copy editor who must be up to her elbows in word polish. She certainly shined up mine. Designer Margaux Keres's layout is so crisp, watch out for paper cuts. My gratitude to two high school friends who smarted-up the book: a bouquet of lilies to Nina Grayson for picking up embarrassing typos and eye-roll examples; every reader should be grateful to Phil Lovelady whose suggestions helped cut the book's word count in half! Kudos to the entire team at Ten Speed/Crown/Random House who design, produce, publicize, sell, and ship this book. Special thanks to JoAnn Gassaway at Random House for answering my pleas to send books ASAP.

I am indebted to all the career professionals I have learned from since the beginning of my career in careers in 1975. Without the work of colleagues and mentors, my contributions to the field would be paltry indeed.

Young adults and parents need to hear about career decision making from many perspectives and many voices. My profound gratitude to all the experts who contributed their sage advice. Very special thanks to the fabulous career coach Robin Roman Wright, friend, colleague, and copublisher. Robin keeps me sane and makes me laugh. And she came up with the best tag yet for skills stories—see chapter 1 for her contribution.

Huge bouquets of thanks to all the young adults I have taught, coached, and counseled. The most helpful bits about career choice for those under twenty-five I learned from them.

With deep gratitude,
Carol Christen

www.parachute4teens.com
E-mail: Parachute4teens@gmail.com
Twitter: @parachute4teens
Facebook: www.facebook.com/parachute4teens

MY PARACHUTE

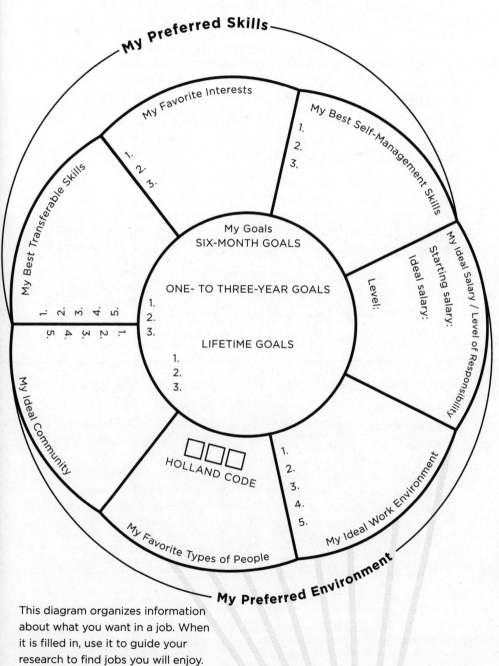

My Preferred Skills

My Favorite Interests

My Best Self-Management Skills
1.
2.
3.

My Best Transferable Skills
1.
2.
3.
4.
5.

1.
2.
3.
4.
5.

1.
2.
3.

My Goals
SIX-MONTH GOALS

ONE- TO THREE-YEAR GOALS
1.
2.
3.

LIFETIME GOALS
1.
2.
3.

My Ideal Salary / Level of Responsibility

Starting salary:
Ideal salary:

Level:

HOLLAND CODE

1.
2.
3.
4.
5.

My Ideal Work Environment

My Ideal Community

My Favorite Types of People

My Preferred Environment

This diagram organizes information about what you want in a job. When it is filled in, use it to guide your research to find jobs you will enjoy. To make it easier to use, photocopy this page and enlarge it.

PREFACE TO THE THIRD EDITION

or Why You Should Want to Read This Book

The querulous career strategist in me wants to assert that you should read this book because I said so. But you deserve a better answer than that. So how about this one: my daughter followed the Parachute process exactly and now has a life she loves financed by work she loves. Is her life perfect? Hardly. Is her life fun, mostly what she wants, and a work in progress? Certainly.

In high school, my daughter was the scholar I was not. No surprise when, as a high school junior, she reiterated her intention of going to college. She'd already announced that plan at age five.

My daughter wasn't surprised when I said that my checkbook was closed until she had a plan for why she was going to college, what she would study, and how that connected her with a career. The summer before her senior year in high school, she did the same Discovery Exercises that are in chapters 1 through 4. She used the information on her parachute (see page vii) to direct her research into jobs and careers that would suit her. Through information interviews she determined what she wanted to study, where she wanted to study, and how those studies would help her pick a career or get a job. She also got suggestions for volunteer experiences and jobs that would help her attain her long-term career goals. Throughout the next few years, obstacles were many. Knowing how greatly she wanted to achieve her goals helped her persevere.

I want the same joy in life and work for each and every teen and young adult in the world. And that is why I want you to read this book.

GET IN TOUCH!

Thanks to all who have written to us sharing your experiences with the first two editions of the book. Authors love to hear from their readers. Your stories help make new editions better. If you would like to share with others your experiences using this book, your thoughts on creating a life or career you love, or a good resource, please e-mail parachute4teens@gmail.com.

INTRODUCTION

Have you had a few part-time jobs already? Maybe you liked your work, maybe you didn't. Perhaps you liked some parts but not others. Work and all your life experiences are valuable because they tell you important things about yourself and about what you want to do.

Ready for an adventure? Great! This book is an adventure that will help you discover what's most important to you. The purpose of this adventure is to answer this important question: How do I find work I will love?

REALITY CHECK

You can do an amazing amount of career work, including reading this book, in just twenty minutes a day.

WHAT CAREER PLANNING IS—AND ISN'T

People who haven't experienced career planning sometimes fear that it narrows down their options by forcing a decision they'll be stuck with. Good career planning—the kind you're going to learn by reading this book—will not narrow your options. *Parachute*'s decision-making process generates more, not fewer, choices.

> Don't worry about failures . . . worry about the chances you miss when you don't even try.
> —JACK CANFIELD, COAUTHOR OF
> *CHICKEN SOUP FOR THE SOUL*

DISCOVER YOUR DREAM JOB
and plot to get it

> Hold on to those dreams of being a firefighter or ship captain or doctor or nurse. Don't let others tell you that those are silly dreams. I think so many people end up doing, consciously or not, what others expect of them, or they settle for less because they think achieving their dream is too hard.
> —ROB SANDERS, PEDIATRIC PHYSICIAN, AGE 28

Do you know what your dream job is? Have you talked with half a dozen people who do that job and know it's a good fit? That's great. If you aren't so sure, that's okay too. Perhaps your dream job will become clear over time, as it does for many people. If being a happy and successful adult is your goal, taking time to search for your dream job is very important. Much of your adult life will be spent working, so having work you love will help make your whole life much more fun.

Surprisingly, the process of finding your dream job can be very fun. You'll become a detective looking for clues in your life and in those of others. You'll uncover what matters most to you, what you love to do, the attributes of people with whom you work well, and where you'd like to live. The Parachute form assembles your clues into a blueprint to lead you to work you'll love.

Many don't find their dream jobs because they assume having their whole dream come true isn't possible. They pursue whatever part might come true. The problem: Whichever part of your dream you pursue, your whole heart won't be in it. You'll pursue that half dream halfheartedly. Half your dream is all that will come true.

We want you to discover and pursue your whole dream with your whole heart!

Part 1 begins your detective work. You'll uncover clues that will answer these three questions:

1. What do you like to do and what are you good at?

2. Who (that is, what kind of people) do you like to do those things with?

3. Where do you like to do those things?

Once you know your what, who, and where, you'll be ready to learn how to find jobs that fit. *How* is more challenging, so it's covered briefly in part 1 and in detail in part 3. But before that, in part 2 we'll look at some things you can do right now to get yourself on your way to your dream job.

> I was lucky—I found what I wanted
> to do early in life.
> **—STEVE JOBS, COFOUNDER AND CEO OF APPLE**

As you explore what you have to offer, with whom you want to work, where you want to be, and how you can get hired in your favorite field, you'll want somewhere to list your most important discoveries. My Parachute on page vii brings your key career-choice information together on one page. The Parachute is divided into categories that will help you organize what you uncover. When you put all your what, who, and where clues on one page, you'll have a clear word picture to guide you in finding work you'll love. Your Parachute diagram is designed to steer you toward a job you'll love.

Keep your career work in both electronic versions (computer, flash drive, external hard drive, cloud) and hard copy. With this backup, you won't lose your hard work should your computer crash. You'll want to return to your Discovery Exercises often to finish your parachute, plan for higher education, or go after your dream job. Your answers will change as you accumulate more life and work experience. People with dynamic careers revisit their parachutes every couple of years.

PARACHUTE TIP

Take your book to a print shop and have it spiral bound. Removing the spine makes the book lie flat so it's easier to read and photocopy.

CHAPTER 1

WHAT YOU LOVE TO DO
your favorite and best skills

Why does this first chapter focus on what you love to do? Because what you love to do reveals your interests and your skills. Those favorite interests and skills, especially the skills that you most enjoy using (which we call your "best" skills), are major clues to finding work you'll love. Let's look at your interests first.

PARACHUTE TIP

Read yacht captain Timothy Forderer's views on the necessity of loving what you do on page 22.

DISCOVER YOUR FAVORITE INTERESTS

Take a moment and think about how you spend your time. Of all the activities you do, which are the most fun? What captures your attention—and your imagination? What is your favorite subject in school? What fascinates you? Everyone will have different answers—his or her unique combination of interests. Danika, for example, loves movies. Jeff spends hours on his computer trying to figure out new ways of doing things. Jessica loves plants and gardening, and Darnel lives and breathes sports—all kinds of sports. So how might these different interests lead Danika, Jeff, Jessica, and Darnel to work they'll love?

Let's take a look at Danika's interests first. If Danika chooses movies (or filmmaking) as a career, she could be an actress, a screenwriter, or a director—or maybe a movie critic (then she'd get to see lots of movies). But Danika has many more possibilities to choose from. She could be a researcher (especially for historical movies), travel expert (to scout locations), set designer, model builder, carpenter (to build sets), painter (for backdrops and the like), costume designer, makeup artist, hairstylist, camera operator, lighting technician, sound mixer or editor, composer (for sound tracks), stuntperson, caterer, personal assistant (to the director or cast members), first-aid person, secretary, publicist, accountant, or any number of other things. The credits at the end of a movie list even more personnel and their roles, although you've got to read fast.

Danika also loves animals and is really good at training them. She could combine her interests and become an animal trainer (or "wrangler" as they're sometimes called) for the film industry. That's a job most people wouldn't think of when considering careers in film.

What kind of career might Jeff's interest in computers lead to? He could be a programmer, computer repairperson, or video game developer. Or because he loves art as well as computers, maybe he'll work with Danika in the film industry as a computer FX designer, web designer, or illustrator of educational materials. These are just a few of Jeff's job options, depending on his other interests and skills.

Jessica, because of her interest in plants and gardening, could become a florist, botanist, or developer of plant hybrids, or she might run her own landscape design, lawn maintenance, or plant nursery business. If Jessica likes to travel, she could be a plant photographer or search for exotic plants to be used in medical procedures.

Darnel's love of sports might lead him to be a professional athlete or a coach; or maybe—because he loves working with kids and has a little brother with cerebral palsy—he might teach adaptive physical education, helping children with physical disabilities get the exercise they need.

As you see, your interests can lead you in many different directions for your work life. It's true that interests change with time, age, and exposure to new people, places, and experiences. But it's also true that your interests now may be with you all your life, so naming your current interests is a great starting place for finding work you'll love. Let's take a closer look at your interests now.

REALITY CHECK

Don't worry about picking your big career-for-life now. It's better to focus on work you will enjoy that can finance your twenties.

DISCOVERY EXERCISE

HOW TO FIND WHAT YOU LOVE TO DO: DISCOVER YOUR FAVORITE INTERESTS

Write your answer to each question on a slip of paper or sticky note.

- When you have free time and no one is telling you what to do, what do you like to do?

- What's your favorite subject in school?

- When you're in the magazine section of your school library or a bookstore, what type of magazine (computer, fashion, sports, news, and so forth) will you pick up and read first?

- Fill in the blank: When I'm _____, I lose track of time and don't want anyone or anything to disturb me.

- If someone asked you what your favorite interests are, what would you say?

- What are your favorite hobbies, sports, or recreational activities?

- What Internet sites are your favorites? What sites do you have bookmarked? What is the subject matter of those sites?

- What kinds of problems do you like to solve?

- What kinds of questions do your friends or classmates bring to you for help?

- What fascinates you? What could you read about, talk about, or do for hours?

After you've answered all the questions, put your answers in a list. Use sticky notes (or experiment with a prioritizing grid at www.beverly ryle.com/prioritizing-grid to make a new list in order of priority (your favorite interest first, second favorite next, and so on). Then write your top three interests in the My Favorite Interests section of My Parachute (page vii). If your interests change, be sure to update your parachute.

Good work! You're off to a great start.

SKILLS YOU ENJOY USING

In this section, the definition of *skill* we are using is an ability or the exper-tise to do something well. Your skills are closely tied to your interests—especially the skills that you most enjoy using. We call these your "best" skills because they are your best clues to finding a job you love. How? It's simple: when you know what your skills are, especially your best skills, you can look for jobs that use them. It just makes sense that the jobs you're most likely to enjoy will use your favorite skills. Once hired, you're more likely to keep your job if it involves your interests and the skills you do well. Why? To succeed in most fields, you have to work long hours. It's hard to succeed if you don't like what you do—you'll want to spend less time at work, not more.

"But I don't have any skills," you say.

Nonsense! You have more skills than you realize. Often our best skills are so close to us that we're not even aware of them. They come so easily and naturally that we think they are nothing special or that anybody can use them the way we do. It's true that you probably don't have as many skills as your older brother or sister has, and older siblings probably don't have as many skills as your parents or favorite teachers have. Our skills grow more numerous as we grow. As we gain more life experience, pursue further education, or work at a particular job for an extended period of time, we gain more skills. But by the time you're a teenager, you've already developed many skills. Let's find your favorites.

Transferable Skills

At its most basic, a skill is a developed aptitude or ability. A skill can range from a basic life skill like being able to turn on a water faucet (which we can't do till we're tall enough to reach the faucet and strong enough to turn the handle) to a more advanced skill like being able to drive a car. Skills are sometimes called *talents* or *gifts*. In this book, we'll use the word *skills*.

There are three different types of skills used in career planning. The most basic building blocks of any task are transferable skills. Along with your interests, transferable skills are the foundation for finding what you love to do. Sometimes they're also called "functional" skills because these are skills you do actively, such as gathering information or data or working with people or things.

REALITY CHECK

It takes a long time to get good at something. You might as well spend that time involved with something that really interests you. Many successful ventures—such as RoadtripNation, Facebook, and Playing for Change—were started by young entrepreneurs following their interests.

Let's say you like to skateboard. (Skateboarding could be one of the interests you named earlier.) When you skateboard, you work with some "thing" (a skateboard), and skateboarding is what you do with the skateboard. What are your transferable skills? You have hand-eye-foot coordination, physical agility, and exceptional balance, as well as the ability to make split-second decisions and take risks. Nothing limits these skills to skateboarding. They'd be valuable in (that is, transferable to) work as a surfing instructor, lumberjack, search-and-rescue crew, or any number of other jobs.

Transferable skills can be divided into three different types: physical, mental, and interpersonal. Physical skills use the hands, body, or both. Physical skills generally involve working with things (such as materials, equipment, or objects, like your skateboard). Working with things includes working with nature (plants and animals). Mental skills primarily use the mind and generally involve working with data, information, numbers, or ideas. Interpersonal skills primarily involve working with people as you serve or help them with their needs or problems. (We use the acronym TIP to refer to all three kinds of skills: Things, Information/Ideas, or People.)

DISCOVERY EXERCISE

HOW TO FIND WHAT YOU LOVE TO DO: IDENTIFY YOUR SKILLS

Scan your mind back over the last month. Did you complete any tasks successfully? What were they? Did you enjoy them?

You begin to identify your skills by looking at your life. Think about projects you have completed, recent problems that you solved, your hobbies, and the activities you do for fun. These can be experiences from your school, volunteer work, paid work, or free time. Select a project or activity you've enjoyed that had an outcome—writing a paper, helping to organize an event, or learning something new, such as a sport or hobby.

Rich Feller, professor of career development and author of the book *Knowledge Nomads and the Nervously Employed*, says that 70 percent of our skills come from challenges, 20 percent from watching others, and 10 percent from classes and reading. Pick a story to write from any of these three categories. If you're stumped about what might make a good skills story, look particularly at challenges you have overcome. Once you've thought of a story, write a short paragraph that describes how you completed your project or worked out a solution to the problem you had. (Need a little inspiration on what kind of story to write? See the Student Example on page 12.)

Now give your project, problem, or activity a title. Then answer these questions:

- **Goal or Problem:** What was your goal—that is, what were you trying to accomplish, or what was the problem you were trying to solve? Any time you have a goal that challenged you, you'll find lots of skills.

- **Obstacles:** What made achieving your goal (or solving the problem) difficult? How did you overcome these obstacles?

- **Time Frame:** How long did it take you to achieve your goal or solve your problem? Using an overlong time frame can often hide skills. If solving a particular problem took several years, pick an especially challenging part of that problem.

- **Outcome:** What happened? Did things go as you expected, or did something unexpected happen?

So if one of your skills is skateboarding, your transferable skills include physical skills (hand-eye-foot coordination, agility, balance, and maneuvering) and mental skills (split-second decision making). Skateboarding can also involve using interpersonal skills, especially if you're on a team or enjoy teaching others how to skateboard.

Why Are My Transferable Skills Important?

Your transferable skills are particularly important as you look for your dream job because they can be moved to any field or career you choose, regardless of where you first picked them up or how long you've had them. For example, your ability to swim is a skill that can be transferred to—or used in—work as a lifeguard, a swim coach, a counselor at a summer camp, or a US Navy SEAL.

As mentioned earlier, transferable skills are the basic building blocks of activities, tasks, or roles used in any job or career. Most jobs rely on certain core activities or tasks that you do over and over. To do these activities or tasks, you need to have certain skills. These groups of skills are sometimes called "skill sets." Why it's so important to identify yours is that if you know your best transferable skills, you can compare the skills needed in a job with those you do well and enjoy using. This kind of comparison will help you find a job you'll love. If a job doesn't use three-quarters of your best skills, you probably won't be happy with it. The more of your best and favorite skills you use in a job, the more likely you will love it.

———— STUDENT EXAMPLE ————

BUILDING A DECK
By Michael Marcinkowski, age 17, high school junior

> My grandfather is a contractor. Last summer, he wanted some projects done at his house. He hired me for a week. One of my projects was to destroy and rebuild a deck. Following my grandfather's instructions, this is what I did.
>
> • Used sledgehammers of various sizes to destroy the deck.
>
> • A two-pound mallet was needed to destroy parts of the old deck.
>
> • Chucked pieces of wood (the old boards) into a pile.
>
> • Put tar paper on the beams using rubber cement.
>
> • Placed the new boards on the supports and nailed them down.

- Some of the two-by-fours were bent. In order to nail these down, my grandfather and I had to nail one side down and use a crowbar to straighten out the board before nailing it in place.

Goal or Problem: Tearing out and rebuilding a deck

Obstacles: Meeting his grandfather's specifications; hard, physical work

Time Frame: A week

Outcome: Old deck hauled away; new deck built

Michael doesn't consider himself a writer. Notice he made a list of what he did to meet his goal. As long as your list includes the details—a step-by-step of how you met your goal, solved a problem, or overcame a challenge—a list of the steps works well for skill identification. The more details you include, the more skills you will find.

Now that you have an idea of what kind of story to write, are you ready for a little detective work to help find your dream job? Good! Let's turn to your life now and begin to identify your skills and, in particular, your best skills.

PARACHUTE TIP

You may want to photocopy the Skill TIP boxes on pages 15 to 17 before you begin marking the skills you used. This leaves you with a fresh copy if you want to do this exercise in the future or share it with a friend.

Discover Your Skills

Now that you've read Michael's Deck Project, write your own story. Reread your story. Make a list of the skills you see that were involved in doing what you did. Look especially at words that end in -*ing*. These words are called gerunds, and they indicate that you are do*ing* something. Now, reread your list of skills for this story and set it aside. Trying to match these skills to the Skill TIP boxes on pages 15 to 17 is beyond frustrating. It's much easier to go the opposite way: look at each skill described in the TIP box and mark box #1 for the ones you used. All of the skills in these boxes are transferable—you can use them in many different settings or jobs.

For example, if you used the skill "making" in your story and what you made was a presentation to your chess club, put a check mark in box #1 underneath "making presentations in person" on the Skills with People page (page 17, third column over, third box down).

Here are a few of the skills that Michael might have used in his deck project.

- **Skills with Things (physical):** using my hands; using hands and eyes in coordination (helps not to nail your finger); motor/physical coordination with my whole body having strength or stamina. [These are just the skills from the first column that Michael used. He would have found more skills in the other five columns of skills with things.]

- **Skills with Information (mental):** Michael used his skill with numbers (measure three times, cut once). If he thought about or wrote out his plan for the deck step-by-step, he would have also used his skills at planning (page 16, second column, last key). Very likely he used the skill of retrieving information when he remembered his grandfather's instructions. Michael would have used his memory to keep track of details.

- **Skills with People (interpersonal):** taking instructions; asking questions for clarification; risk taking. [Working for a relative always is!]

Now that you've gone through the process and understand how it works, write four more stories so you have a total of five. If you wrote about a project the first time, try writing about something else: teaching your little sister how to ride a bike, learning to ice-skate, dealing with a friend who gossiped about you behind your back. The reason you need five stories is the same as why soil samples are taken from a variety of different places from a tract of land. Five stories help you dip into different parts of your life and see what skills are there. This number also lets you see how often you use particular skills. Do they show up in four or five stories?

You've already written skills story #1. Next, for story #2, place check marks in box #2 for each skill. Do this for each of the remaining stories, #3, #4, and #5. You will find that in each story, you used many different skills— some in the "things" category, others in the "information" category, and still others in the "people" category. If you write one story a day and fill in your skills, then in five days you can know what your best transferable skills are— and you'll have two sections of your parachute done!

When you have all five stories written and their skills marked, look over the Skill TIP pages. Is one page loaded with skills, or are your skills spread evenly over all three pages? Each person's skill patterns are different. Don't worry if yours don't look the same as those of your best friend.

SKILLS WITH THINGS

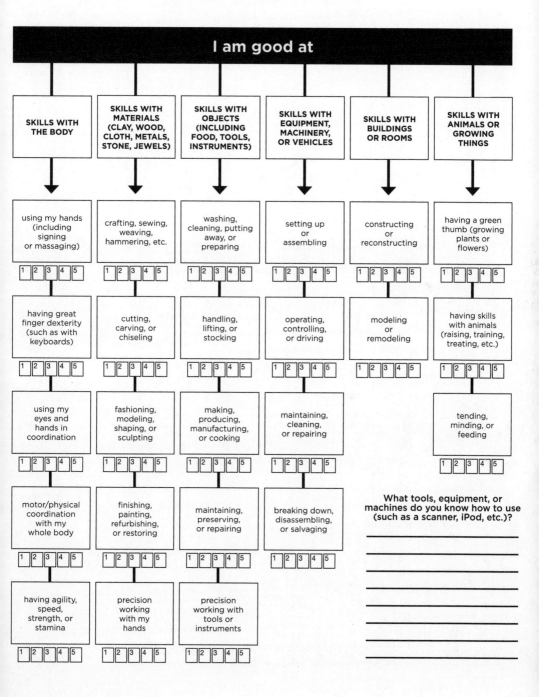

I am good at

SKILLS WITH THE BODY	SKILLS WITH MATERIALS (CLAY, WOOD, CLOTH, METALS, STONE, JEWELS)	SKILLS WITH OBJECTS (INCLUDING FOOD, TOOLS, INSTRUMENTS)	SKILLS WITH EQUIPMENT, MACHINERY, OR VEHICLES	SKILLS WITH BUILDINGS OR ROOMS	SKILLS WITH ANIMALS OR GROWING THINGS
using my hands (including signing or massaging)	crafting, sewing, weaving, hammering, etc.	washing, cleaning, putting away, or preparing	setting up or assembling	constructing or reconstructing	having a green thumb (growing plants or flowers)
1 2 3 4 5	1 2 3 4 5	1 2 3 4 5	1 2 3 4 5	1 2 3 4 5	1 2 3 4 5
having great finger dexterity (such as with keyboards)	cutting, carving, or chiseling	handling, lifting, or stocking	operating, controlling, or driving	modeling or remodeling	having skills with animals (raising, training, treating, etc.)
1 2 3 4 5	1 2 3 4 5	1 2 3 4 5	1 2 3 4 5	1 2 3 4 5	1 2 3 4 5
using my eyes and hands in coordination	fashioning, modeling, shaping, or sculpting	making, producing, manufacturing, or cooking	maintaining, cleaning, or repairing		tending, minding, or feeding
1 2 3 4 5	1 2 3 4 5	1 2 3 4 5	1 2 3 4 5		1 2 3 4 5
motor/physical coordination with my whole body	finishing, painting, refurbishing, or restoring	maintaining, preserving, or repairing	breaking down, disassembling, or salvaging		
1 2 3 4 5	1 2 3 4 5	1 2 3 4 5	1 2 3 4 5		
having agility, speed, strength, or stamina	precision working with my hands	precision working with tools or instruments			
1 2 3 4 5	1 2 3 4 5	1 2 3 4 5			

What tools, equipment, or machines do you know how to use (such as a scanner, iPod, etc.)?

_____

_____

_____

_____

_____

_____

_____

SKILLS WITH INFORMATION

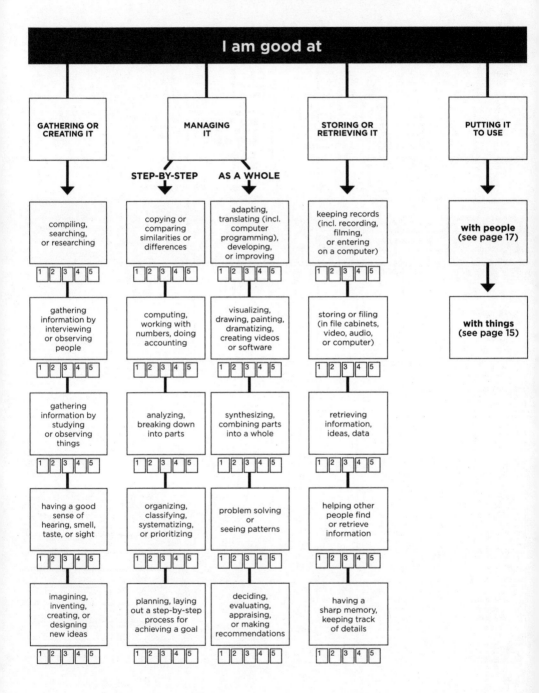

I am good at

GATHERING OR CREATING IT

compiling, searching, or researching

1 2 3 4 5

gathering information by interviewing or observing people

1 2 3 4 5

gathering information by studying or observing things

1 2 3 4 5

having a good sense of hearing, smell, taste, or sight

1 2 3 4 5

imagining, inventing, creating, or designing new ideas

1 2 3 4 5

MANAGING IT

STEP-BY-STEP

copying or comparing similarities or differences

1 2 3 4 5

computing, working with numbers, doing accounting

1 2 3 4 5

analyzing, breaking down into parts

1 2 3 4 5

organizing, classifying, systematizing, or prioritizing

1 2 3 4 5

planning, laying out a step-by-step process for achieving a goal

1 2 3 4 5

AS A WHOLE

adapting, translating (incl. computer programming), developing, or improving

1 2 3 4 5

visualizing, drawing, painting, dramatizing, creating videos or software

1 2 3 4 5

synthesizing, combining parts into a whole

1 2 3 4 5

problem solving or seeing patterns

1 2 3 4 5

deciding, evaluating, appraising, or making recommendations

1 2 3 4 5

STORING OR RETRIEVING IT

keeping records (incl. recording, filming, or entering on a computer)

1 2 3 4 5

storing or filing (in file cabinets, video, audio, or computer)

1 2 3 4 5

retrieving information, ideas, data

1 2 3 4 5

helping other people find or retrieve information

1 2 3 4 5

having a sharp memory, keeping track of details

1 2 3 4 5

PUTTING IT TO USE

with people (see page 17)

with things (see page 15)

SKILLS WITH PEOPLE

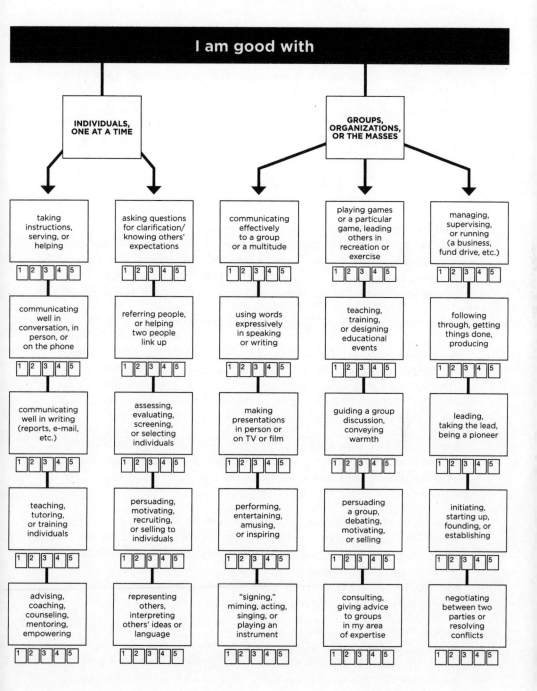

I am good with

INDIVIDUALS, ONE AT A TIME

taking instructions, serving, or helping
1 2 3 4 5

communicating well in conversation, in person, or on the phone
1 2 3 4 5

communicating well in writing (reports, e-mail, etc.)
1 2 3 4 5

teaching, tutoring, or training individuals
1 2 3 4 5

advising, coaching, counseling, mentoring, empowering
1 2 3 4 5

asking questions for clarification/ knowing others' expectations
1 2 3 4 5

referring people, or helping two people link up
1 2 3 4 5

assessing, evaluating, screening, or selecting individuals
1 2 3 4 5

persuading, motivating, recruiting, or selling to individuals
1 2 3 4 5

representing others, interpreting others' ideas or language
1 2 3 4 5

GROUPS, ORGANIZATIONS, OR THE MASSES

communicating effectively to a group or a multitude
1 2 3 4 5

using words expressively in speaking or writing
1 2 3 4 5

making presentations in person or on TV or film
1 2 3 4 5

performing, entertaining, amusing, or inspiring
1 2 3 4 5

"signing," miming, acting, singing, or playing an instrument
1 2 3 4 5

playing games or a particular game, leading others in recreation or exercise
1 2 3 4 5

teaching, training, or designing educational events
1 2 3 4 5

guiding a group discussion, conveying warmth
1 2 3 4 5

persuading a group, debating, motivating, or selling
1 2 3 4 5

consulting, giving advice to groups in my area of expertise
1 2 3 4 5

managing, supervising, or running (a business, fund drive, etc.)
1 2 3 4 5

following through, getting things done, producing
1 2 3 4 5

leading, taking the lead, being a pioneer
1 2 3 4 5

initiating, starting up, founding, or establishing
1 2 3 4 5

negotiating between two parties or resolving conflicts
1 2 3 4 5

Summary: Discover Your Skills

1. Write and reread a story.

2. Identify the skills you used.

3. Make a list of the skills you used.

4. For each skill of the Skill TIP boxes, pages 15 to 17, ask yourself, "Did I use this skill in accomplishing my goal?"

5. If this is your first story, check box #1 for each skill you used. Second story? Check box #2 and so on until you have identified the skills used in each of your five stories.

IDENTIFY YOUR BEST TRANSFERABLE SKILLS

Now we're ready to find which skills are your "best" ones—the ones you most enjoy using. Every job will include some tasks or need a few skills you don't much care for. But to find a job you'll enjoy, you want to know which skills you really like to use and which ones you do well. Think about big chunks of time. What skills do you like enough to use over and over all day long?

You have both "can-do" and "want-to" skills. Can-do skills are ones you don't want to use very often. They come along with you, and you may even need to use them in your dream job. But they're not the focus of your work. For example, you probably have the skills to wash all the dishes from a Thanksgiving dinner for thirty people. You may have used your dishwashing skills daily. But how often would you want to use those skills at your job—all day, every day, once a year, never?

Want-to skills are ones you enjoy using and could do over and over again, several times a day, and not go crazy. It's important to remember that each of us has different can-do and want-to skills. The world needs people with different skills.

Look at the Skill TIP pages again. Which are can-do and which are want-to skills? Cross out your can-do skills—that is, any skills you *can* do but don't really *enjoy* using. It might be hard to cross out some of your can-do skills if you are very good at using them and have gotten kudos for using them in the past. Cross them out anyway. You don't want to build a career around can-do skills. This will bring you little joy in your work.

Now, the really fun part: finding your best skills. Go back to the Skill TIP boxes. Of the skills that you like to use and that you used in more than one story, select ten that you most enjoy using. Write each one on a slip of paper or sticky note. Look at each skill. Think about how much you want to

DISCOVERY EXERCISE

IDENTIFY YOUR BEST TRANSFERABLE SKILLS

1. Review your list of skills used. Cross out skills you don't really like using.

2. Select ten skills you enjoy using.

3. Put the skills in order from most favorite to least favorite.

4. Look at your list of ten skills. The top five are your best transferable skills.

5. Write those skills in the My Best Transferable Skills section of My Parachute (page vii).

IDENTIFY YOUR BEST SELF-MANAGEMENT SKILLS

Reread your five stories at the same time. It will take you just a minute or so per story.

1. What traits or self-management skills did you use in your stories?

2. What similarities do you notice? Do you see any patterns in how, or how often, you use your favorite skills? (Don't worry about being right. Guesses are okay.)

3. Write each trait on a separate sticky note.

4. Organize the sticky notes in order of priority, with your favorite and most important trait first and so on. Once you've found the right order, make a separate list of these ranked traits.

5. Write your top three traits in the My Best Self-Management Skills section of the My Parachute diagram (page vii).

As a young worker, you may not have many specific kinds of knowledge or work-content skills, but if you are dependable, punctual, and work well with others, you can get hired based on your self-management skills or traits.

use that skill. Do you want to use it often or only occasionally in your work? Place these ten skills in order from your most favorite to your least favorite. This can be hard, but give it a try. (If you'd find it helpful to use an online prioritizing grid, go to www.beverlyryle.com/prioritizing-grid. You'll find instructions for filling out and using the grid.) When you know your best transferable skills, you have an important clue for finding work you love.

Teens and young adults frequently ask if they have to be experts to keep a particular skill on their lists. No. If you like using the skill, have a moderate amount of experience with it, and marked it in several stories, keep it on your list of favorites. Remember, it's always possible to develop your skills more fully through education, practice, or concentration.

Now, look at the top five: these are your best and most favorite transferable skills. They are an important part of your parachute. Write these five skills in the My Best Transferable Skills section of My Parachute on page vii. (Feel free to use colored pens or pencils to add a little color to your parachute!)

For a quick summary of these steps, see "Identify Your Best Transferable Skills" in the Discovery Exercise on page 19.

IDENTIFY YOUR BEST
SELF-MANAGEMENT SKILLS

Neat categories always have exceptions. In your stories, you may have some bits that don't fit into the Skill TIP boxes, but you think they might be skills. They probably are! You actually have three different kinds of skills.

Transferable skills are also called functional skills. If something functions, it works. When you work, you're using your transferable skills. The five stories you write and check off on the Skill TIP boxes help you discover what your favorites are.

Knowledge skills are revealed through your interests. If either math or construction is an interest of Michael's, he knows fractions, decimal points, and how to read a tape measure. Knowledge skills are also known as *work-content skills*. These skills are what you must *know* in order to do a certain job or activity. To engage in most of your interests or hobbies, you have to have knowledge specific to that activity. For example, a friend of yours knows Slovak and is often called upon to translate what grandparents are saying for younger cousins. Slovak is one of her knowledge skills.

Knowledge skills can be found in interests you already have or those you want to study further. You filled these in under My Favorite Interests on My

Parachute (page vii). Your interests involve specific skills that could be useful for your career. If you uncover additional interests through your stories, should you add them to your original My Favorite Interests list and reprioritize that list? That depends on how much you want a particular interest to be part of your work. Spend some time thinking about each of your interests, and divide them into two categories: *Fascinates me* or *Doesn't fascinate me*. Prioritize only those that fascinate you.

Self-management skills are also known as personal traits. These traits describe the unique way you use your skills or how you manage yourself in relation to other people. Adventuresome, thorough, energetic, decisive, and compassionate are all self-management skills. Michael had a desire to help his grandfather and earn some money. This might be a sign that he is ambitious. Michael finished the deck within the allotted week, showing that he is dependable. If Michael showed up and worked on his projects without his grandfather reminding him, then he is self-motivated. All of these traits are valued by employers and will help Michael in his career. Self-management skills are clues about the work environments and people you need to be surrounded by in order to be efficient, productive, and successful. Go to the Discovery Exercise on page 19 for instructions on how to identify your top choices for self-management skills.

Well, that's done! I hope you had fun, too. Now you know three different kinds of skills that can help you get and keep a job you'll enjoy—favorite interests, best transferable skills, and best self-management skills—and you've recorded them on My Parachute.

The Discovery Exercises guide you in uncovering and naming what you need to do the very best work you can. Did you learn something about yourself that you didn't know before? Did an exercise confirm something that you sensed?

PARACHUTE TIP

You can learn more about self-management skills and their importance to your future career by doing an Internet search. Use the phrase "self-management skills" for your search.

Now that you know what you love to do, awaiting in the next chapter are discoveries about what types of people you like to have around you when you do what you love to do.

EXPERT ADVICE

WHAT'S LOVE GOT TO DO WITH WORK?

By Timothy Forderer, yacht captain
www.timforderer.com

My name is Timothy Forderer, and I'm a professional yacht captain. I manage a ninety-foot private sailing yacht that is currently circumnavigating the world. In the last twelve years, I've sailed over 130,000 miles. I'm writing this while anchored in Antarctica, surrounded by glaciers and penguins. We have giant albatross birds with wingspans of nine feet swooping by the yacht, curious seals popping their heads for a look at us, and minke whales shooting random water spouts all around us. I Do What I Love!

Sound AMAZING? It is.

This yacht has been my home and *my job* for the last nine years. I'm working with an amazing person who shares my passion for visiting very remote destinations. My dream has come true.

Find your passion! When I was 8 years old my dad taught me to sail, and I took to it like a fish in water. I was lucky—I found at an early age what I loved to do. From that point on I was obsessed with learning all I could about sailing. I had no idea where this was going to take me in life, but I trusted my inner voice and my heart, and I followed my interest vigorously.

No matter what, don't lose sight of your dreams! My life took a turn and I needed to quickly get a "real" job. I found a job in the cellular phone business and gave it my all. I spent the next eleven years wearing a suit and tie and climbing the corporate ladder. During this time I kept my sailing dream alive—it was still there in my heart. I would notice it in the feeling I would get looking out the office window and watching a puff of wind dance across the pond.

Live each day as if it were your last! When I was thirty-five, we went on a family sailing trip to the British Virgin Islands. My dad pulled me aside, put his arm around me, and somberly told me that this would be the last time we would sail together. Two months later I held my dad's hand as he took his last breath and died of cancer of the throat.

This was a serious wake-up call for me. I realized the clock was ticking, that I was not invincible, that I would die one day. This is what it took for me to follow my dreams and turn my passion into my career.

I ask myself often, "If today were the last day of my life, would I want to do what I am about to do today?" Whenever the answer is "no" for too many days in a row, I know I need to make a change.

I'm so convinced that Doing What You Love is the secret to a happy and fulfilled life that I've made it my personal mission to talk with high school students all over the world. Visit www.dwylmentors .blogspot.com to see me in action and learn more!

The secrets to making your dreams a reality:

• Be careful what you wish for . . . because it WILL come true.

• Be careful what you do not wish for . . . because it WILL NOT come true.

• We attract into our life a direct reflection of what we have inside our hearts and minds, so stay positive and focused on your dreams.

• Choose work that's important to you and that you care about, and you will be fulfilled and help make the world a better place.

TIPS FOR TEENS AND YOUNG ADULTS WITH ADHD

By Robin Roman Wright, BCC, career and ADHD coach
coachrobin@leadershipandcareers.com
www.linkedin.com/in/adhdcoachrobin

If you have ADHD, you may be wondering if you can use the Parachute method for finding a dream job. I have worked for many years with teens and young adults with ADHD, and I can confidently say, "Yes, you can." However, you will be more likely to complete this book's activities if you strategize with a trusted adult. This can be a parent, relative, teacher, guidance counselor, career center counselor, or career coach.

When thinking about career planning, one important thing to keep in mind is that school is likely the most restrictive environment in which you will ever have to perform. Many work environments allow for more individual approaches to completing assignments, some room for negotiating working conditions and project delivery dates, and even flexible schedules.

The US economy is evolving and changing quickly, providing opportunities for people with the ability to think outside of the box—as many with ADHD do. Individuals with ADHD often have a creative spark, keen interests, and a bountiful curiosity that helps them succeed in the workplace.

Extracurricular activities are of particular importance for teens and young adults with ADHD. These are avenues where you can develop competence and really shine. Experts agree that it's best for people with ADHD to work in a field that fascinates them, so notice and nurture what interests you! Many of these areas and activities will be passing interests and may become future hobbies, but one or two may open doors for you to shine in a future line of work.

> The youth of today need to be prepared from an early age for what lies ahead. It starts with the system guiding a young person to focus on areas where he has natural abilities, not because he is lazy and doesn't want to get challenged but because this is an area he is naturally wired for and we don't want him/her struggling later on in life.
>
> —YUSUF OLANREWAJU, 30-YEAR-OLD HUMAN RESOURCES PROFESSIONAL (DEGREE IN GUIDANCE AND COUNSELING), NIGERIA, WEST AFRICA

A HERO'S APPROACH TO CAREER CALLING

By Carolyn Kalil, college counselor and author of *Follow Your Inner Heroes to the Work You Love*
www.linkedin.com/pub/carolyn-kalil/2/944/a0b

Who are some of your heroes? A hero is someone who goes out and achieves great deeds on behalf of a group or the world in general. His or her true strength does not come from the outside world; it comes from within. When you look inside and identify your unique strengths and talents, you too will discover your true greatness and make a contribution to the world.

The most important step in finding this strength is to know who you are—not who you were told you should be, but who you truly are. Once you can answer this, you will have the key to taking a hero's approach to your dream job.

There is no one way to be a hero because no two people are alike. We all have different strengths. Look at the symbols within the triangle below to get clues about what kind of person you are.

 I am a HELPER. My heart rules my head. My strength is in my ability to emotionally connect with others. I am warm and friendly and am often referred to as a people person. I experience a great deal of joy in supporting and inspiring others to succeed.

 I am a THINKER. My head rules my heart. I love to analyze things. I receive great joy in dreaming up new ideas. I am a visionary and problem solver.

 I am a PLANNER. I am organized. I am the one who shows up early and stays late. I am responsible, practical, and dependable. I value family and tradition.

I am a DOER. Don't expect me to sit around thinking about something. If you want something done now, send it my way. I need adventure, fun, and excitement in my life. I am a spontaneous and courageous risk taker.

How would your life be different if you allowed yourself to be like your heroes? How can you use your unique strengths to help others? Your answers will put you on a path of being the hero of your life and finding the kind of dream job that matches who you already are.

Author's note: Watch a few Pixar movies. Study the heroes and superheroes in these films. Which types of heroes do they represent? Helper? Thinker? Planner? Doer? What qualities do they share, and which are unique to a particular character?

CHAPTER 2

WHO YOU LOVE TO WORK WITH
your favorite types of people

Have you had a part-time or summer job where your work was pretty boring but you still liked going to work? Did you like going to work because of the people? Did coworkers become friends? Maybe you had a boss who was friendly and helped you learn new skills, or you met interesting customers, clients, and patients every day. If you haven't had a job yet, you may have had similar experiences in a class—it wasn't super-exciting but your friends were there, the teacher made the subject interesting, or projects took you outside the classroom to meet amazing people.

Short of being a total hermit, most every job you'll have as a teen or early twentysomething will surround you with people. Later in your career, you may work from a home office or even out of your suitcase and laptop as you travel the world. A good job can be ruined if you work with difficult people or people with whom you're not comfortable. But an ordinary, not-so-interesting job can be fun if you enjoy your coworkers.

Finding a dream job involves more than discovering what you love to do; it also means discovering what kinds of people you enjoy. Let's do that now by going to a "party"!

THE PARTY

You've received an invitation to a party of people your age or a little older. You don't know any of them well. "What kind of party is *that*?!" you wail. Don't worry; we promise it'll be fun.

Below is an aerial view of the room where the party is happening. Guests with similar interests have gathered in different corners of the room. Every group is filled with fascinating people chatting with each other.

The terms Realistic, Investigative, Artistic, Social, Enterprising, and Conventional (R-I-A-S-E-C) tag each corner. The aerial diagram gives brief descriptions of the people who might be attracted to each letter group. Examples of their specific interests appear on page 28. You'll notice how their interests and skills all work together.

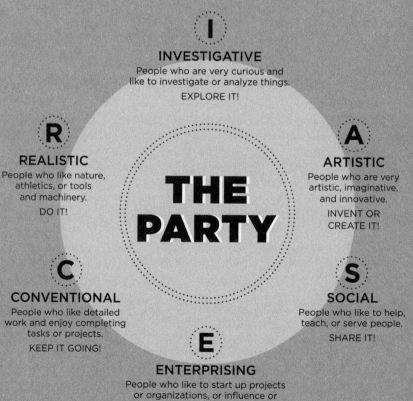

I

INVESTIGATIVE
People who are very curious and like to investigate or analyze things.
EXPLORE IT!

R

REALISTIC
People who like nature, athletics, or tools and machinery.
DO IT!

A

ARTISTIC
People who are very artistic, imaginative, and innovative.
INVENT OR CREATE IT!

THE PARTY

C

CONVENTIONAL
People who like detailed work and enjoy completing tasks or projects.
KEEP IT GOING!

S

SOCIAL
People who like to help, teach, or serve people.
SHARE IT!

E

ENTERPRISING
People who like to start up projects or organizations, or influence or persuade people.
START IT OR SELL IT!

Realistic (R): People who like nature, athletics, or tools and machinery. *Examples:* Tom loves to hike in the mountains and does volunteer trail maintenance. Dee plays on the school soccer team. Paul repairs cars. Louise and Larry build furniture in their father's woodworking shop. Ross grows vegetables for the farmers' market, and Yvette raises dogs to be companion animals for people with disabilities.

Investigative (I): People who are very curious and like to investigate or analyze things. *Examples:* Jason always wants to know why—why a certain bird is no longer seen in his area, why the brain works the way it does, why one ball team plays better than another. Jessica investigates the best places to take a date—concerts, movies, amusement parks, hiking trails—and writes about them for her school paper. Erin analyzes everything—from the data in her chemistry experiments to the results of community-service projects. David, a student council member, wants to figure out why new students have so much difficulty scheduling the classes they need.

Artistic (A): People who are very artistic, imaginative, and innovative. *Examples:* Ashley draws cartoons. Carlos, Aaron, and Stacy started a band and play at local dances. Guy designs costumes and sets for school theater productions and is known for being able to create great stuff with few resources. Daniela develops her own software for doing computer animation.

Social (S): People who like to help, teach, or serve people. *Examples:* Isabel, a senior, orients first-year students about life at high school. Steve tutors middle school students in math and English. Keri volunteers at a food bank. Darin is a trainer for the school football team. Bob serves as a peer counselor.

Enterprising (E): People who like to start up projects or organizations, or influence or persuade people. *Examples:* Dana started a service project where high school students visit the elderly in a convalescent home. Ty, who's running for student-body president, persuades people to vote for him. Greg got some of his friends interested in working with kids who are at risk of getting involved with drugs and gangs.

Conventional (C): People who like detailed work and enjoy completing tasks or projects. *Examples:* Michael, the treasurer for a service club, keeps detailed financial records of all its fund-raising activities. Kristin works part-time in an insurance office, where she's responsible for keeping all the files up to date. Terri oversees the preparations for the prom, making sure everything that needs to get done gets done.

Okay. Now you know a little about who'll be at the party. You've just arrived. You walk in the front door. (Don't worry if you're shy or don't know what you'd say if you talked to anyone. That doesn't matter at this party.) Now, we have three questions for you:

1. Which corner of the room would you go to first—that is, which group of people would you most enjoy talking to for the longest time? Write the letter for that corner in the box.

2. After fifteen minutes, everyone else in the corner you chose leaves for another party. Of the groups that still remain, which group would you be drawn to the most? Which people would you most enjoy being with for the longest time? Write the letter for that corner in the box.

3. After fifteen more minutes, this group also leaves for another party. You look around and decide where to go next. Of the groups that remain, which one would you most enjoy being with for the longest time? Write the letter for that corner in the box.

The three letters you selected indicate your "Holland Code." The Holland Code is named for Dr. John Holland, a psychologist who did research on "people environments"—that is, the types of people we most like to be with. Dr. Holland's research showed that everyone has three people environments they prefer among these six—Realistic, Investigative, Artistic, Social, Enterprising, and Conventional. The three groups of people you'd prefer to talk with at this party give clues as to your favorite people environment.

Turn back to My Parachute (page vii) and write your Holland Code in the section My Favorite Types of People. Then write a short description of your code on a separate sheet of paper. Is your Holland Code *IAS*? You might write: "I'll enjoy my work if I'm surrounded by people who are very curious and like to investigate or analyze things (I), who are highly innovative and creative (A), and who want to help or serve people (S)." Include details from My Favorite Interests. Your description will give more clues to work that suits you.

The Party exercise actually provides just an approximation of your Holland Code, but it's been found to be accurate by 90 percent of those who complete it and then take the more comprehensive Self-Directed Search (SDS) assessment. Go to www.self-directed-search.com to take the SDS online. It takes twenty to thirty minutes, and is a real bargain at ten dollars. You can print out a personalized report listing the occupations and fields of study that most closely match your interests. You'll be on your way to finding out your ideal work environment!

Look over the traits for each of your top three groups. Do you see yourself in the descriptions? You can see yourself better by looking at others; this is called the Mirror Theory. When we describe the people we would most like to be with, in many cases we have also described ourselves. An old saying that describes this phenomenon is "birds of a feather flock together." What do you think?

CAREER ASSESSMENTS

This book is designed to take the place of career assessments by exposing clues from your experience. But if your school offers career assessments that you can take for free as part of a career class or career center orientation, take advantage of the opportunity. If your school doesn't have a career program or hasn't offered you any assessments by the time you are fifteen, you can find a few inexpensive or free options online, including the SDS mentioned on page 29.

REALITY CHECK

There are several ability tests (as opposed to interest assessments) available to teens and young adults. All cost money and some cost a great deal. The Armed Services Vocational Aptitude Battery, better known as the ASVAB, is available through many high schools for free. It is a very high-quality ability test. Make sure you've thought out your feelings about serving in the military in advance of taking the test. If you score high in abilities needed by any branch of the military, recruiters can be intense and insistent in their efforts to sign you up. You can be flattered, but you needn't be persuaded. All branches of the military offer higher education as a perk for enlisting, which makes joining enticing, but military life is not for all young adults. Make sure you can say, "Thank you, but I'm not interested," if that's how you feel.

Talking with an adult can help you better understand your career planning. If you get along well with your school guidance counselors, show them your parachute or the results from assessments you've taken. If your school guidance counselor doesn't have time for brainstorming or is the last person whose opinion you'd seek, it's great to discuss your parachute and assessments with one of your career mentors.

Assessments do have limitations, especially when it comes to naming your best skills. Another reason why a filled-in My Parachute diagram is so important!

No assessment can give you a final, once-and-for-all answer about what job would be perfect for you. But assessments can give clues as to where you should begin the search for your dream job among the thousands of possibilities. In the United States, there are currently thirty thousand job titles at work. Technology and consumer demand create more new jobs every month.

While assessments would ideally begin with all thirty thousand jobs and then narrow down the territory for you, few assessments use more than five hundred jobs in their databases, so any list of suggestions you get is very limited. The jobs suggested are those chosen in the past by people who answered the assessment's questions the same way you did. However, these suggestions are a good place to begin your investigations. Do some research on the Internet or in books like the occupational guides in a library: learn a bit about each job that's suggested before nixing it. Don't get discouraged if there aren't any suggestions you like. Do a little bit of thinking. In what field are the jobs that were suggested for you? Does this field interest you, even if the particular jobs suggested don't? Might there be other jobs in this field that would use all your skills or that match your parachute well? Through research and networking (which we'll explore later in the book), you can home in on jobs you'll enjoy.

More Dream-Job Clues

Your Holland Code, the three letters you chose in the Party exercise, tells you what type of people you enjoy being with and provides clues to jobs you might enjoy. If your three letters are RIA (Realistic, Investigative, Artistic), you may find being a police sketch artist or occupational therapist of interest. If your letters are SEC (Social, Enterprising, Conventional), you might enjoy working as a self-employed wedding planner or an event coordinator.

You can explore more job possibilities at www.cacareerzone.org. If you take their Quick Assessment, you'll get a Holland Code and a list of job titles that match yours. This site is for jobs in California and there is no national site quite like it, but if a job sounds like it fits you, you can do some research to find out whether there are similar jobs where you live (or hope to live).

You can also use your three-letter Holland Code to research job possibilities at www.onetonline.org/find/descriptor/browse/Interests/. Through either CaCareerZone.org or O*net sites, you may discover interesting jobs you might never have thought of doing, or jobs you never knew existed. This career research expands your job possibilities.

CAREER SITES FOR FURTHER EXPLORATION

Another fabulous free site is www.cacareercafe.com, designed for California students considering going to community college. If you don't live in California, find out if your state has similar learning or work opportunities. The site has free assessments (under START), information about professional organizations, suggested courses of study, career planning and job-search tips, and so much more. You can connect with CaCareerCafe.com on Facebook, Pinterest, and Twitter.

EUREKA.org is one of the largest career information sites in the English-speaking world. EUREKA provides assessments, information about two thousand different jobs, links to colleges and universities where you can pursue your studies, and advice for your parents. The site has a variety of job-search resources, including lists of short-term and two-year courses of study that prepare you for high-wage, in-demand jobs. It's a secure site to store information for your career plans.

Your high school or college may subscribe to EUREKA—check with your career center or guidance counselor to see if EUREKA is available to you. If not, get a few friends together and chip in toward a month or two at twenty dollars per month. The EUREKA website is worth every penny!

BOSSES AND CLIENTS

What is your idea of a good boss? Knowing the attributes of good bosses makes them easier to recognize should you come across one. A good boss can be a great mentor. Teachers are very much like bosses. Some of them make you work very hard, but they manage to pull good work out of you, and you learn a lot from them. When you are just starting out, you want a boss from whom you can learn to be excellent in your field, trade, or craft.

- Make a list of characteristics of a good boss for you.

- Prioritize the list.

- If you envision yourself in a job where you have customers, clients, or patients, list what kind of people you'd want them to be. Want to be a speech pathologist working with children and teens? If you work in a hospital setting, your *patients* would be children and teens. If you work as an independent speech consultant, your *clients* would be children and teens.

- Prioritize this list as well.

- Write your top two or three descriptors from both prioritized lists into the My Favorite Types of People section of the My Parachute diagram (page vii). If there's no room, draw a line and write along the bottom of the page.

CHAPTER 3

WHERE YOU LOVE TO BE
your ideal work environment

Your heart has its own geography, where it prefers to be. That may be by a mountain stream. It may be in the Alps. It may be in the hustle of the streets of Shanghai or New York. It may be on an Oregon farm. It may be a beach town. Or it might be right where you are now—in your own home-town or in your own backyard.

REALITY CHECK

Geography has become ever more important for making career plans. In the United States, one in three young adults doesn't want to move away from the area in which she or he grew up. The job market these adults must explore is the one in which they now live.

Why prepare for jobs located somewhere else? Dynamic economies with ever-expanding job opportunities thrive on both coasts of the United States. Texas, the Dakotas, and parts of the upper Midwest are also hopping job markets. Markets with demographics that include an abundance of young entrepreneurs and recent college graduates are where new jobs are born, as well as where plenty of openings in already existing occupations are found.

Your heart knows the places that it loves. Finding where you most want to live is as important as doing what you love. Imagine having your dream job, but in a place you abhor—not a pretty picture. Living and working where you are happy is an important part of your dream life. It's living your whole dream, not just half or less. This chapter will help you find that place.

There are lots of ways to consider where you want to live. We'll explore two: your ideal work environment and your ideal community. We'll be asking you lots of questions. You may have answers to some and none to others. That's okay. Answer what you can and just keep the rest of the questions in the back of your mind. Questions you can't answer can actually be useful, making you notice new things and examine possibilities in a way you hadn't before. If asked, "Would you rather work outside or indoors?" and you aren't sure, you may start to notice what types of jobs are done indoors or outdoors, or what jobs combine both indoor and outdoor work. You might think about how you feel after being indoors for several hours compared to spending the same amount of time outside. Maybe you want to work indoors, but on weekends you prefer to be mountain biking, hiking, skiing, or surfing.

Answers you know are clues to guide further exploration of where you'd love to live, work, and play. Your answers will change over time as you visit places you've never been before—going away to school or working several jobs in different locations will expand your ideas about what makes certain geography a good fit for you. Through experience you learn what, who, and where is most important in your life. Let's start by exploring something you may never have thought about before: your ideal work environment and what makes it just right for you.

YOUR WORK ENVIRONMENT

If you get a full-time job, roughly one-quarter of your life each week will be spent at work. Some young adults have gotten their ideal job using their best skills, only to find that the workplace is so uncomfortable they must quit. Your work environment needs to be one in which you not only feel comfortable but also can thrive. We use the term "environment" here because your ideal "where" includes more than just the location (office, laboratory, farm) where you do your work. Your work environment also includes your work space (desk, cubicle, lab space, five-thousand-acre ranch, or machine shop); physical conditions (windows or no windows, natural or fluorescent lighting, noisy or quiet); atmosphere (formal, casual, lots or little interaction with people, working style); company size (small, large, local, national, international); and clothing (uniform, suit, jeans, or the latest fashions).

When you've visited various workplaces, such as your parent's office, your doctor's office, or your school, what have you liked or not liked? Where do you like to study—in a quiet library or in your bedroom with the CD player on, alone or with a group? Where do you feel comfortable or uncomfortable? Where would you like to spend more time? The same job (or very similar jobs) can happen in many different environments—some you would love, some you would hate! Let's explore what's right for you.

MY IDEAL WORK ENVIRONMENT

Answer the following questions as best you can, but don't feel that you need to answer them all at once. Set a timer for fifteen minutes. If you're enjoying the exercise when the timer goes off, set it for another ten minutes. Or answer some of the questions now, then come back again in a week and answer some more. The second time around, you may notice things that you weren't aware of before. Think of something not included here? Put that on your list, too.

Location: Where would you most like to work . . .

- Indoors or outdoors? In an office building? In a machine shop? On a ranch? At your home?

- In an urban, suburban, or rural area?

- In many locations or one spot (travel or no travel)?

Work Space: What kind of space would you most enjoy . . .

- A cubicle in a large room with lots of other people in their own cubicles?

- Your own desk in a private office?

- Lots of variety—at a desk, in your car, at clients' locations, on airplanes, in hotels?

- A classroom, laboratory, hospital, garage, workshop?

- Outdoors—golf course? ranch? barn? forest? under the sea?

- A place with everything you need—all the latest tools or technology and necessary supplies—or a place where you need to be creative with limited resources, supplies, and equipment?

Physical Conditions: Do you prefer . . .

- Fancy and upscale, moderately nice, or does it not matter?

- Windows that open and close or a climate-controlled building?

- A light or dark environment? Natural or artificial light?

- Comfortable temperature or varied temperatures?

- Safe or risky? (What does "safe" mean to you, and what might you need to feel relaxed and able to do your best work?)

Atmosphere: Do you prefer . . .

• Noisy or quiet? Calm or bustling?

• Formal or casual—for example, do you want to call your coworkers "Ms. Smith" and "Mr. Jones," or do you prefer that everyone is on a first-name basis?

• Lots of contact with coworkers or very little?

• Lots of contact with the public (clients, patients, customers) or very little?

• A hierarchical setting (where the boss tells everyone what to do) or a collaborative setting (where the staff works together to determine goals, priorities, and workload)?

Size/Type of Business: Do you prefer . . .

• Large or small? (Think about what "large" and "small" mean to you.)

• Locally owned, national, or multinational? For-profit or nonprofit organization?

• Knowing all your colleagues and customers or always having a chance to meet someone new?

• Running your own business?

Clothing: What would you like to wear at work . . .

• A suit?

• Trendy clothes?

• Casual, comfortable clothes?

• A uniform (for example, military, firefighter, police officer, waiter/waitress)?

• A lab coat?

• Whatever you want to wear?

Answer enough questions to gather a list of ten items, aiming to include at least one from each category—Location, Work Space, and so on. Write each item on a sticky note, and rank them by importance. Select your top five factors, and write these in the My Ideal Work Environment section of My Parachute (page vii).

YOUR IDEAL COMMUNITY

You and your friends have different ideas of what makes a great place to live. Ski fanatic? You'll want to be within easy distance of the mountains. Love to surf? A surfing community on the coast will suit you. One friend may want to live near a lake, river, or desert. Another may want to live near good friends or family. Do you have excellent foreign language skills (or want to develop them)? You may want to live in a foreign country.

More directly related to jobs are transportation issues. Want to work within a few blocks of mass-transit stops? Need to drive to work, requiring ample parking possibilities? How about biking or walking? Want your gym or favorite coffee bar nearby? A grocery store on the route home? A park close enough for lunch or a stroll? What characteristics do you want in the community where you'll live and work? Go to the Discovery Exercise on page 40 for instructions on how to identify your ideal community.

YOUR IDEAL SALARY AND LEVEL OF RESPONSIBILITY

To fill in this section of your parachute, you'll explore the level of responsibility you want, along with your level of compensation. This is the first section on your parachute where we will be looking at two different time frames: soon and in the future.

How much responsibility you take on will affect whom you interact with and in what ways. How much money you want to make can strongly influence where you live: salaries vary wildly depending on geography or supply and demand, and these realities can turn your ideal location into not so ideal.

A job finances your life. What level of financing do you want? You'll need numbers for starting salaries and for wages of experienced workers. See the Parachute Tip on the opposite page for recommended salary websites. Keep in mind that salary information is often very general, as career literature usually quotes national averages or median salary. Double-check all compensation information with mentors or people who work in the industries, fields, or locations that most interest you.

People routinely brag about what they paid for an item, but most—even parents—are mum about what they earn. Asking people "What's your salary?" or "How much do you earn?" is taboo. If you keep your questions away from their personal earnings, people will help you get accurate salary information. You can ask a less direct question, such as "The average starting salary for this job nationally is $31,750 a year. Are local starting salaries similar?"

The force that drives salaries up or down is supply and demand. If there is a great supply of workers with certain skills, but little demand, the salary for that work will be low. Salaries rise when there aren't enough workers (supply) to meet demand. The ideal situation is to find jobs that you like a lot and that are in high demand. If you can't find both, your challenge is to figure out whether it's more important to you to have a steady income (doing something you enjoy less) or to work in a field that absolutely fascinates you (but doesn't pay as well). If you have to make a choice, this book is here to help you figure out your priorities. Go to the Discovery Exercise on page 41 to figure out your ideal salary and level of responsibility.

REALITY CHECK

Teens and young adults often have unrealistic ideas about salaries. In a study done by Accenture Consulting, only 18 percent of 2014 college grads expected to earn less than $25,000 a year, while 41 percent of 2012–2013 employed college grads reported that their annual salary was $25,000 or less.[1]

The median wage in the United States is $27,500. Median means half of the people working earn less than that number and half earn more. Check out what your fantasy lifestyle will cost at www.cacareerzone.org/budget or www.jumpstart.org/reality-check.html.

1   David Smith, Katherine LaVelle, and Anthony Abbatiello, *Great Expectations: Insights from the Accenture 2014 College Graduate Employment Survey* (Accenture, 2014), http://www.accenture.com/SiteCollection Documents/PDF/Accenture-2014-College-Graduates-Survey.pdf.

MY IDEAL COMMUNITY[2]

Geographical Features: Do you want to live . . .

• In or near the mountains? near the coast? in the desert? on the plains?

• In a small town (fewer than 5,000 people), a medium-sized city (5,000 to 20,000), a large city (20,000 to 500,000), a major metropolitan area (500,000 or larger)?

• In a rural area with a town or city within a reasonable distance, or in an isolated area far from "civilization"?

People: Do you prefer . . .

• A good mix of age, ethnic, economic, and religious groups?

• Mostly people your own age or in your own ethnic, economic, or religious group? Living where you already have friends or family or in a place where everyone is new?

Neighborhood/Housing: Do you prefer living . . .

• In an apartment or condominium?

• In a subdivision? In a single-family home that doesn't look like everyone else's?

Culture: What is important to you . . .

• Good bookstores, art galleries, libraries, and museums?

• Movie theaters? Music, dance, and the arts?

• A local semipro or pro sports team?

Educational Opportunities: What is important to you . . .

• Personal enrichment classes? Professional development classes?

• A college or university?

Recreation: What would you like your community to have . . .

• Good parks? Bike paths, walking/hiking trails?

• Community sports leagues and facilities?

---

2   The categories and items on this list are not your only choices. We hope these suggestions will stimulate additional ideas about what makes a community ideal for you. Don't overlook brainstorming with a group of friends to get more ideas.

Commuting: What is important to you . . .

- Commute by car?
- Ability to take mass transit to work?
- Being able to walk or bike to work?

Write the answers to these questions on small slips of paper or sticky notes and arrange them in order of their importance to you. Select the top five characteristics and write them in the My Ideal Community section of My Parachute (page vii). Like using an online grid? Go to www.successonyourownterms.com/prioritizing_grid.htm?items=10&.

MY IDEAL SALARY AND LEVEL OF RESPONSIBILITY

Do you want to earn as much money as you possibly can? Or is your goal to earn just enough to take care of yourself, save a bit, and have time for hobbies and friends? Ask yourself,

- What salary do I want to make when I get out of school?
- What salary do I need to finance life in my twenties?
- What salary do I hope to be making after five years of experience?
- What do I want my top salary to be?
- What jobs that interest me pay what I hope to earn?

Research online and by contacting people familiar with the jobs or fields in which you intend to work. What compelling jobs pay what you'd like to earn now and in the future?

Write your rock-bottom starting salary and your ideal salary on the My Parachute diagram in the section labeled My Ideal Salary (page vii). This is your salary range. Will your ideas about salary change over time? Undoubtedly. But this is a great start.

What level of responsibility appeals most to you? Do you want to be an employee, salesperson, supervisor, or manager? Do you want to own the place? What is the "level of worry" you want to take on? If you don't want the worries of work to follow you home, choose your level carefully. If you manage your career well, though you may start out at one point— entry level supervised by others—over time you can gain the education and experience to advance to a supervisor position yourself.

Briefly summarize what level of responsibility you want and write that on your My Parachute diagram (page vii).

CHAPTER 4

YOUR PARACHUTE DESCRIBES YOUR DREAM JOBS

It's very hard to find something if you don't know what you're looking for.

The Discovery Exercises you did in the preceding three chapters are pieces of your career puzzle. Filled out and prioritized, the My Parachute diagram (page vii) is a word picture that describes the job components you seek. With a little more investigation, the pieces will come together to become crisp images of possibilities for your career direction.

Try not to narrow your options for your dream job too quickly. Humans are more comfortable with labels than puzzles, but don't lock yourself into a job title without looking at all the opportunities to use your best skills and favorite interests—you might pass by a dream job and never know!

> I wish I had known that there were opportunities to earn a comfortable living much closer to the types of dreams and interests that I had in high school. I was an avid lover of maps back then. Had I known that being a cartographer was an available career, I would have fervently pursued it.
>
> —ADAM HOVERMAN, DO, FAMILY PRACTICE PHYSICIAN, AGE 30

TRANSFORM INTERESTS INTO FIELDS

The process of finding potential dream jobs can involve a little "translation": taking your favorite interests and determining occupational fields in which they fit.

If skateboarding is an interest, fields to consider might be athletics, recreation, kinesiology (the study of the principles of mechanics and anatomy in relation to human movement), or mechanical or materials engineering. In the field of athletics, you might become a skateboarding coach. In recreation, you might create skateboard teams or a program for new skateboarders. If you combine kinesiology with engineering, you might design skateboards that are safer to use or more flexible for maneuvers. The training or education you need varies according to the field you pick.

Here's another example. Tamara wants to be a nurse. Her top interest is medicine. Her best skills are taking care of sick or injured people. Tamara is good at math and science (especially chemistry). The kind of nurse she becomes depends on what type of training she completes, what major she chooses, and what her other interests are.

The field of medicine is quite broad. Here are some of the nursing jobs Tamara could pursue:

• If she wants to work with children, she could be a pediatric nurse. Pediatrics is the specific field in which she'd use her nursing skills.

• If cancer care is a strong interest, Tamara could be an oncology nurse. (Field = oncology)

• In emergency medicine, Tamara could be an emergency room nurse, work on a search-and-rescue team, or be part of a Life Flight medical team. (Field = emergency medicine)

• In recreation, she could be a nurse on a cruise ship or at a large resort. (Field = recreation)

The same job happens in many different fields, some of which you'd like and some you'd hate!

PARACHUTE TIP

The words *career* and *job* are often used interchangeably. You can usually determine the meaning of the word by its context. "Your career" generally refers to your total time in the world of work, and is made up of a series of jobs in a related field. To build your first career path, you will learn about jobs, careers, and professions. Expect that as your knowledge of a career field intensifies, your job goals will change.

EXPLORE DREAM JOBS

With your interests translated into fields, it's time to find dream jobs in those fields. Do you already have an idea of what those jobs may be? Great. If not, here are steps you can take to discover dream jobs to explore:

• Show your parachute to people whose opinions and suggestions you trust. Can they suggest job names for you to research?

• Read tons of information about different occupations. Ask reference librarians or career center staff to direct you to resources that will help you find jobs that fit your fields of interest and your skills. County OneStop career centers and websites (online at www.careeronestop.org/) have materials about job demand in your county. Industries and occupational fields often have websites that give information about available jobs.

• Do an Internet search to find information about specific jobs or careers.

• Keep an eye out for jobs mentioned in magazines, blogs, or TV programs that interest you enough to investigate.

• Find people who work or have worked in fields that intrigue you. Talk with new hires and well-established workers. Recent retirees are also good sources of information, especially about the long view.

• If you want to continue living in the same region where you currently live, get in touch with local people doing fascinating work. Read on to find out how!

CAREER-DEVELOPMENT TOOLS

Filled in your parachute? Read about jobs that are a dream fit? You should be able to name three different fields or jobs that might match your parachute. Now it's time to meet people working in those fields or jobs—this is one of the best ways to find out what careers might suit you. Accurate pictures of what these jobs entail can emerge from these meetings, especially if you meet at the work site.

In career exploration and job-search classes, this informal research goes by many names. You'll hear it called networking, field research, informational interviewing (quite the tongue twister), and other phrases. Essentially, it's gathering information you need for career planning by bringing helpful people into your orbit. We'll call it *network building* and *information interviews*.

DISCOVERY EXERCISE

TRANSLATE INTERESTS INTO FIELDS

1. Turn to My Parachute, page vii. Look at the section entitled My Favorite Interests.

2. Take your list of favorite interests to your library or look at websites like www.onetonline.org/find/family. Find names of fields (also called *job families*) that seem to match your interests. List two or three fields for each interest.

3. List these fields on your parachute or in a separate document or journal.

You can get help from parents, school counselors, librarians, or career center staff to complete this exercise. Keep in mind that it's fine to start with guesses. Your research into jobs in each field or family that interests you will help you uncover precise names for those that fit you best.

> Curiosity turns work into play.
> —PAUL GRAHAM, CREATIVE TECHIE AND BLOGGER

Network Building

The older you get, the more you'll hear the word *networking*. Not everyone understands the point of networking. They're so busy collecting contacts (in the business world, people are labeled *contacts*), they forget the goal: to build a professional network that can share resources and make things happen. Want to find a new veterinarian, new dance club, or new job? Network building expands your connections to people who can help you find what you seek. Building networks is a tried-and-true career-choice and job-search strategy. Your options for jobs, colleges, courses to take, and skills to learn are greatly enhanced by your proficiency in network building.

Network building can be done formally or informally.

Informal network building happens when you want to learn more about an issue, hobby, or activity. Ever ask someone where he bought his cool shoes? Have you tried to find an extra ticket to a must-see concert? You've done informal networking.

So has Jesse: Jesse likes to build and fly remote-control model planes. He's got a summer job working for eight weeks at a residential camp that's a six-hour round-trip drive from home. Jesse is going to take a couple of planes

PARACHUTE TIP

Don't have much experience of pleasant conversations with adults? Stressed out at the thought of talking to an adult about her work? Through practice information interviews, you can pick up interviewing skills. Talking about something you enjoy isn't intimidating. What are your favorite hobbies or activities? Is there a building in town you've long wanted to visit? Pick one or two things you're so interested in or knowledgeable about that you could talk to *anyone* about them, and then do just that—with a friend's mom, a parent's friend, or a teacher. Do make your last practice interview with someone you don't know. This will help you face your fear of talking with strangers; something you'll do a lot of throughout your work life.

If you do two to five of these practice interviews, you'll learn what it feels like to have a conversation about a strong interest. Once that feels comfortable, move into information interviews.

with him so he can fly them when he's not working. He's hoping to convince the activities director to let him start an interest group with the campers. He has written plans for one to three hours of activities. Jesse wants to find other people in the area who fly model planes, because if his group is approved, having the campers meet other enthusiasts would be awesome. How can he do that?

• Jesse asks members of his model club if they know of a club near the camp or anyone in that area who flies model planes.

• At his hometown hobby store, Jesse learns there's a regional club near the camp, but no hobby store. Jesse now knows that he'll need time to make a list of parts for a group and for his own planes to bring with him.

• Jesse takes with him a booklet of instructions he downloaded from the Internet. It explains how to build a landing strip for power model airplanes, since he found out by talking to a regional club member that there isn't one near the camp.

Formal network building is more focused. Information interviews are an example of formal networking. Your focus is to gather information about current conditions and trends in specific fields or jobs. You can use them to get ready for a job hunt or a round of dream-job investigation.

PARACHUTE TIP

Wondering if information interviews are lame, terrifying, or pointless? Get your hands on *Make Things Happen* by Lara Zielin (Lobster Press, 2003). This book is short, fun, and easy to read. In just one hundred pages, it lays out the lowdown on how and why to do information interviews and network building. The book has a great explanation of the ever-dwindling Six Degrees of Separation and how degrees of separation affect job hunting.

Getting hired is still a people-to-people activity. Whether you make your contacts through Internet connections or former coworkers, you'll find more job opportunities via formal networking than through want ads in any media. Through your network, you can

• Gain a realistic view of a job from someone actually doing it every day.

• Determine if a work environment suits you.

- Meet people attracted to a job or profession to see if they share your values.

- Learn new jargon, trends, and issues.

- Find mentors and leaders in the field or industry.

- Hear about better or faster ways to get job qualifications.

- Set up a Twitter account for your career, and follow the old giants and the up-and-comers you like.

A necessary tool for living, network building is a skill at which you will want to excel.

Information Interviews

Information interviews are opportunities for you to gather information for career decisions by talking to someone doing the job. A trusted adult can help you find people who have jobs you're curious about. Find jobs or people through directories, the Yellow Pages, or the Internet, or by sending requests through Facebook, LinkedIn, Pinterest, Instagram, Twitter, or any other social networking site to which you belong. (See chapter 8 for details on using social media to network.)

Talk to at least three people with a particular job or career before you decide to cross it off your list. Each person's experience with a job is different, so it's best to triangulate to gather the most accurate and balanced information.

You can do some of these interviews over the phone. Even better is interviewing people at their work sites so you can compare their work environment to your ideal. No career decisions should be made without seeing the work setting.

Safety tip: Especially if you're under eighteen, don't feel that you have to go alone to an information interview, even if someone you trust made the recommendation. You can do your interview over the phone or with a video call. If you can't get an interview companion, always meet at a work site when other people are around.

Information Interview Guidelines
With whom do I talk?
Speak with a worker actually doing the job that interests you. This person's boss may be easier to find, and you may need to talk with the boss to get connected with the person who does the job you want information about. But don't stop with the boss. You need to know what it's like to do the job from an employee perspective.

Will I need an appointment?

Probably. If the jobs that interest you are in retail stores or fairly public businesses or places, you may be able to walk in at a slow time and find someone who will talk with you. "What's it like to work here?" is an easy way to get someone talking.

If the job or organization you want to learn more about is farther than a couple of bus stops away or limits public access, or if the person you want to talk with is usually very busy, you'll need to make an appointment for a fifteen- to twenty-minute conversation. You can make the appointment by phone or e-mail.

What do I say to make an appointment?

Develop a "pitch." Write a short script to introduce yourself to the person you'd like to interview. Here's a sample:

> *Hi, my name is Megan. My father gave me your name because you own a mobile pet-care business. I like animals very much. I'm collecting information about pet-centered businesses. Could I make an appointment to talk with you about your work? I'll need about fifteen minutes of your time.*

People may want to know more about you. Be ready to add information about who you are, how you picked them, and why you want to talk with them. This needn't be a soliloquy, just a few additional seconds of information.

What if I freeze on the phone?

Type out your script. Have it in front of you when you make calls. Brain freeze? Quickly refer to your script.

Can I contact someone first with a note?

In the sales field, contacting someone unknown is termed "a cold call." If you find cold calling intimidating, your first contact can be in writing through snail mail or e-mail. You'll need an exact physical or e-mail address. Mention that you will follow up with a phone call to set up an appointment, and be sure to make that follow-up call. Here is a sample of a written request.

Dear Amanda Ruiz:

My name is Taneesha Jones. I am studying mechanical engineering and robotics at Tidewater College. My robotics teacher showed me an article on bionic limbs that you wrote for LiveSience.com. My ultimate career goal is to assist in creating new medical equipment so that people regain their mobility after spinal injuries. I hope to work for a year or two before transferring to a university.

I know you must be very busy, but I am hoping you can spare twenty minutes to talk with me about your work. I would appreciate your suggestions as to what entry-level jobs I might qualify for and what college major might best prepare me for future jobs.

If you would reply with some convenient times to phone you for an appointment, I would be very grateful.

Sincerely,

Taneesha Jones

Will someone see me?

Yes. Not everyone, of course. If you speak courteously when requesting an appointment, communicate clearly what information you're seeking, and show gratitude for your contact's time, eight out of ten people you phone will make an appointment to see you.

People love to talk about themselves. Also, most of them remember being in high school and not having a clue about how to choose a career or get a job. Adults will be impressed that you're doing research now to learn about jobs that will be a good fit for you. Those who are impressed will be very helpful.

If your interviewee likes what he does and likes talking about it, you may find it hard to keep your appointment to its original time limit. It helps to tell your interviewees at the beginning that you have five or six questions. To keep your appointment within the agreed time, keep in mind that they have just two minutes per question. Should the interview run over time despite your efforts, your interviewee may invite you to stay a bit longer. Try not to take up too much of his time.

When you go for the interview, be sure to show up on time and be organized. Have your questions ready. Come prepared to take notes.

Why will someone see me?

As a high school student researching career goals, you've got the *Wow* factor. You are sure to hear, "Wow, I'm so impressed you're doing career research so young" or "Wow, I wish I had done this kind of career investigation when I was your age."

Do I have to go alone?
No. If you're under eighteen, you shouldn't go alone. If you're over eighteen, you can have a trusted adult go with you until you feel comfortable doing information interviews on your own. (Of course, this is not true of hiring interviews! A potential employer would frown upon that, questioning your self-sufficiency.)

Consider taking a friend with you; joint information interviews are valuable if both of you want to know about the job or field. Choose someone who knows how to behave in business situations and who won't embarrass you. It's good business etiquette to ask the person you're interviewing if she minds an additional person joining you. Don't just show up with someone else.

What should I ask the person I'm interviewing?
Your research will have generated questions you want to ask. New questions may come to mind during the interview. That's great! Along the way, make sure you ask the same questions at each interview so you can compare like information to like information. That's an absolute necessity for good research.

Ask the following five questions in every information interview you do:

1. How did you get into your job? What kind of training or education did you get?

2. What three to five tasks do you do most often? How often? What skills are necessary to do these tasks?

3. What do you like about your job? What don't you like about your job?

4. What changes are predicted in your field in the next five to ten years?

5. Do you know someone else doing this (or similar) work with whom I could talk? Are you comfortable providing contact information?

As you listen to the person's answers, take notes. Divide the information into the same categories as those on your parachute.

Interviewing a veterinarian? In response to your question, "How did you get into your job?" Dr. Kelly answers, "I've loved animals since I was a little kid. I always had cats, dogs, birds, horses, and all kinds of other pets. Whenever one of them got hurt, I'd calm it down, clean out the wound—if it wasn't too serious—and help it heal. Math and science are my favorite subjects. I always thought it would be great to be able to help animals all the time when I grew up, so I became a veterinarian."

In her answer, Dr. Kelly told you about her interest in animals and the skills she used working with them. So in Dr. Kelly's parachute, under My Favorite Interests, you would write "caring for animals," "math," and "science." Under My Best Transferable Skills, you'd write "calming animals and cleaning their wounds."

Later, Dr. Kelly mentions that it's important for her to work with people who are compassionate and who love animals (My Favorite Types of People). Does Dr. Kelly say why she chose to become a large-animal veterinarian? Does work with large animals keep her outside, which she loves (My Ideal Work Environment)? Does she live in a rural area where people—ranchers, cowhands, farmers—work with animals for a living (My Ideal Community)?

Dividing information into your parachute categories makes comparisons easy. Where does your parachute overlap with hers? Where does it differ?

To students just starting to reach out for contacts, the most important question asked is the last one: "Do you know someone else doing this (or similar) work with whom I could talk?" Dr. Kelly might give you the name of a small-animal, zoo, or racetrack veterinarian or a veterinary surgical technician. Each name gives you an additional contact. With two or three names from each person you interview, you'll soon have a huge network for learning about jobs you might like. Treat your contacts well and they may help you with a later job search.

The Job Meter

It makes no sense to interview additional people when it's clear you are no longer interested in the work they do. Let's say that after interviewing Dr. Kelly and another veterinarian, you decide that seven years of higher education is not for you. A couple of years of education sounds perfect. Your math and science grades are good. Being a veterinary technician for your first career path is very appealing. There are many different kinds of veterinary technicians, so you interview several of them to see what kind sounds most interesting and fulfilling. Voilà! You make a decision.

If, after an information interview or two, you know that a particular career doesn't float your boat, how do you find people whose work suits you better? The Job Meter can help you formulate questions that will lead you to jobs that better match your parachute.

The Job Meter is the creation of Marty Nemko, PhD, a brilliant, creative career consultant and author. The Job Meter helps you construct questions that uncover work that is closer to your parachute. (For more ideas, visit www.martynemko.com.) Here's how:

1. Listen to someone describing his job. Compare it to your parachute and your hopes. Give the job a rating on a scale of 1 to 10 (1 = awful; 10 = perfect).

2. For ratings lower than 8.5, ask yourself, "What would have to be different about this job in order for it to be a 10?"

3. At the end of your interview, describe how the job of your dreams differs from his job. Do so without sounding rude—remember that he does this work every day. Don't say, "Your job sounds really awful!" or "I'd hate to do this work!" Instead, describe the qualities you'd prefer. Want less people contact and more use of your skills at estimating? You would ask your interviewee for the names of jobs with those features. Does he have names for you? Is he willing to give you contact information? Remember that people's professional contacts are part of their net worth. Handle them like treasure.

4. As you perform more interviews, keep ranking, describing, and adjusting until you find your cache of dream jobs.

JOB METER STORY

Eric is seventeen. Last week he did an information interview with Steve, a stockbroker.

Eric gave that job a rank of 3 on his Job Meter. It did involve math, analysis of information, and using numbers as a reasoning tool—Eric's favorite skills. On the minus side, Steve worked in a high-rise downtown, the work environment was very formal, and his colleagues—who looked stressed-out—worked in tiny cubicles. None of this appealed to Eric.

Today Eric is meeting with his mom's cousin Leah. She's barely thirty and has her own small business as a certified public accountant (CPA). She works in an old house that's been converted into office suites. The surrounding neighborhood has big, leafy trees and outdoor cafés. Leah's workplace feels much more comfortable to Eric than the stockbroker's office. After listening to Leah describe what she does, Eric told Leah about the Job Meter. Eric asked Leah what rating she'd give her job.

"A 9.9," she flashed back at him. "What do you think of it?"

Eric hesitated, "Maybe a 5 or 6. My teacher said an 8 is the lowest number for a career target."

Luckily, Leah wasn't insulted. She smiled and asked, "For you to give it a 10, how would my job have to be different?"

"I'm not sure I want to have my own business or lots of people as clients. I'd like to use my math stills to gather information and write reports that would go to a boss or one client. Tax season seems like doing one report per client. Both you and Steve, the stockbroker I interviewed last week, spend a lot of time meeting new people. I guess that's to expand your business?"

"Yes. I belong to a service club, a community business group, and a women's professional organization. I review the annual taxes for the preschool my son goes to, and I've volunteered to be the treasurer for the co-op kindergarten he'll attend next year. I like to think I'm more subtle than wearing a button that says, 'I'm a CPA and I need your business,' but I'm constantly looking for ways to meet people who may need my services."

"I don't think I'd like that part, constantly meeting new people. I'd also like my day to be split between working inside and outdoors."

Leah thought for a while, then said, "I've got clients who do all kinds of different jobs. Give me a week. I need to check with them to ask if I can give you their names. I'll find people for you to talk with about careers that use math."

"Thanks, Leah. I appreciate your help," Eric responded. Of course, Eric followed up by sending Leah a thank-you note.

Writing a Thank-You Note

After each information interview, always send a thank-you note. Why?

When you meet with people or interview them about their work, they give you something very valuable that everyone has too little of—their time. By sharing their work experience with you, they have given you career information, perhaps even wisdom or a new contact. A gift deserves to be acknowledged, especially a gift you asked for! Information that uncovers a dream job or keeps you from making an inappropriate career decision is a valuable gift. The people you interview will appreciate being thanked for their time. Those you have thanked will be inclined to help you again. Here are some of the reasons to preserve each new contact:

• Would you want this person to be one of your career mentors?

• Is this a job or field you'd like to explore further?

• Might you want to ask this person more questions in the future?

• Might you like to job shadow or do an internship here?

• Will you need letters of recommendation for your job-search portfolio?

Get your interviewee's business card. If a gatekeeper, receptionist, or administrative assistant was helpful or encouraging, get his or her business card as well, and write a second thank-you note.

Does your interviewee not have a business card? Take care of recording contact details at the beginning of your interview. Ask for her job title, the correct spelling of her name, and the contact information she wants to give you. Send a note of appreciation to every person you interview, even if you are not in love with the work they do. You never know whom you might cross paths with again, and who could end up being helpful down the line.

PARACHUTE TIP

To e-mail or to snail mail? That question is batted back and forth between recruiters and career counselors when discussing thank-you notes. There are good reasons to use either or both methods. Just write them!

Thank-You Note Tips

After you leave the interview, make an outline of what you appreciated or learned while it's still fresh in your mind. Three tips while writing your note:

1. Keep it simple. A thank-you note can be just two or three sentences.

2. Proofread and sense check a bazillion times to avoid errors that could make you look unprofessional.

3. Send right away. A thank-you note that arrives a week later seems like an afterthought, not genuine gratitude.

Here's a sample thank-you note:

Dear Mr./Ms./Dr. _____ :

Thank you for talking with me this morning about your work. The information you gave me about work/study and apprenticeship programs is very helpful. I very much appreciate that you were willing to take the time to meet with me.

If I have further questions, may I contact you again? If you are too busy but could refer me to a colleague, I would be most grateful.

Sincerely,

Your Name

Most people send out typed or e-mailed thank-you notes. Handwritten card? Maybe. If your handwriting is atrocious, don't. If it's good, sending a card through the postal service can be a nice way to reinforce your interest and your name. E-cards are another option. Avoid cutesy or vulgar cards—you are writing a note to a businessperson, not a friend.

PARACHUTE TIP

No matter what form of thank-you note, be sure to

- Use standard English (don't write in all caps or all lowercase).
- Use proper punctuation and grammar (no run-on or stream-of-consciousness sentences).
- Run the spell-check tools multiple times.
- Ask an English geek friend or an adult to proofread the note. Spell-check is helpful, but your eyes and brain can be fooled.

The Internet is an ever-refreshing pool of great images and card possibilities. There are websites with wonderful, creative cards, websites with free images, websites with traditional business stationery, and apps to make your own professional-looking stationery.

Did you discover that you share an interest in nature photography? Make one of your stellar photos into a thank-you card. If you and your interviewer share no common interests, focus your note on the company and the job. At the very least, that's your overlapping interest. People appreciate thank-you notes of any kind. Getting a thank-you note totally makes someone's day.

DO YOU NEED A CAREER COACH?

Career coaching can help high school students learn more about the types of jobs they would like to prepare for or college majors they might pursue. A coach can guide you in discovering your marketable skills, identifying your fields of fascination, and determining viable post–high school options more quickly than working by yourself. A coach will carefully listen to your wants, needs, and goals. During coaching sessions, the coach will use questions, written exercises, and feedback to help you make informed decisions about your first career path. To learn more about what a career coach can do, visit www.youthleadershipcareers.com.

AND THEN . . .

When you've discovered three to five jobs that hit high on your Job Meter, make a prioritized list. File it in hard copy or on your computer with your other job-search materials.

To gather that list of three to five jobs that fascinate you, expect to do twenty-five information interviews. If you've done twenty-five information interviews and don't have a list of jobs that fill your occupational dreams, either your parachute doesn't truly reflect what you like or you're not making career choices that make *you* happy. This is a clue that it's time to give some deeper thought and consideration to what you really want for your future.

If more than nine months have gone by since your last job search, review your parachute. Update the components of your dream job to find more satisfying summer jobs, internships, or part-time work, or to help you choose a course of study that can point you in the right direction.

Do you see why it's recommended that you begin basic career planning before you leave high school? You have many contacts at and through your school, from favorite teachers to booster clubs to local employers. Remember your *Wow* factor: adults will open lots of doors to high school students that they won't open for college students.

Kudos for getting this far! You've done a lot of good work discovering what skills you love to use, who your favorite types of people are, and where you'd like to work and live. We hope you've discovered some things about yourself that you didn't know and confirmed some things you did.

The discoveries you've made about yourself in part 1 establish the foundation for the practical steps you can take to land your dream job, presented in part 3. But first, in part 2 we'll take a look at getting the most out of high school and college, as well as some other tools that can get you further down the road toward finding the career that's right for you.

WHAT IF MY DREAM JOB IS WORKING FOR MYSELF?

One-third of the workforce is self-employed, whether or not that's their first choice, and this percentage will grow over time. In any job market, fair or foul, you need to know what kind of business you could start that would give you an income stream quickly.

Under the age of 32? There are more entrepreneurs in the millennial generation than in any previous generation since the Industrial Revolution.

You may like to tinker, have an idea for how to make something better, or want to provide a service that is needed in your community. People who set up their own businesses for profit are called *entrepreneurs*. People who establish a nonprofit to provide services to a special population or target a special issue are called *social entrepreneurs*.

Entrepreneurial and social entrepreneur wannabes can find related articles, blogs, associations, summer camps, competitions, and success stories on the Internet and in books. While you are living at home is a great time to create your own business, like the eleven- and nine-year-old brothers who created a math game app for iPhones. Write a brief business plan. Research how you would start and grow a business. Try it out—you will be that much closer to your dream job and life.

part two

_____

ON THE WAY TO YOUR FUTURE
help if you don't know where to go

High school students need encouragement to seek out
careers that build on what they love to do already. So often
salary, prestige, or ambition gets in the way of chasing
after the golden key to what already motivates and inspires.
Feel the freedom to go in the direction that your dreams
move, however and wherever that freedom is found.
—ADAM HOVERMAN, DO, FAMILY PRACTICE PHYSICIAN, AGE 30

Does it seem that the future is far away? Does working at what you love to do seem like a fantasy? If you do nothing now, hoping that looking the other way will somehow improve your options, you are likely to graduate and have no idea how to turn your career fantasies into a real job. But there are steps you can take to help that fantasy become your life. Right now—this moment, this week, this year—you are creating your future.

Chapter 5 covers ways to make the most of your high school years and use them to get closer to your dream job. Chapter 6 tells how you can use college or life after high school productively to prepare for work you'll love. Chapter 6 includes relevant information about higher education for all kinds of learners. Chapter 7 is about goal setting and achieving. (Goals are tools that will help shape your future *and* get you through this school year!) Chapter 8 is a new spin on an old tool: using social networking sites for career exploration and job search.

Consciously using your high school and college years as part of your career development while learning new tools will give you the skills to convert life and work dreams into your reality.

> The power of vision is extraordinary.
> —DEWITT JONES, AWARD-WINNING *NATIONAL GEOGRAPHIC* PHOTOGRAPHER

CHAPTER 5

WHAT DO I DO NOW?
make the most of high school

Asked if they had regrets about high school, most adults say they didn't make good use of their time to investigate post–high school options that really fit what they wanted.

This needn't be your regret. As you enter and move through high school, think out what you want to do in high school and what you want high school to do for you. You might want to

• Explore your abilities with languages, music, science, art, sports, or leadership.

• Pursue an apprenticeship, an internship with a local employer, or the military.

• Get ready for college.

• Learn enough skills to support yourself after graduation so you can take a break from being a student for a while.

• Gain expertise to find a fun job to finance your life while you figure out your next career path.

• Make time to explore each and every job or career that interests you.

• Become fluent in a language and use your new skills to travel.

Once you know what you want out of three or four years in high school, it's much easier to make year-by-year plans to achieve your goals. You can always add to your goals or change them as you go along. Starting out with a focus for your time in high school ensures that you won't just float along and later regret your missed opportunities.

Students know that to succeed, they need reasonably good grades. Adults look for this sign of academic maturity. But most students don't know the importance of *career* maturity. From ages fifteen to eighteen, they must be making career decisions and creating a plan for how to achieve career and life goals. Both types of maturity are necessary for college and career readiness.

Strategic planning is what successful companies do. You need to do it, too. How you do it is with a detailed plan that you research thoroughly. You can do this by yourself, but it might be easier if you get adults to help you.

A detailed plan? Really? Studies of young adults—whether or not they continue on to higher education—show that those who achieve life and career ambitions had a detailed plan. A plan reminds students why they are in school and how their classes relate to their future. Rather than giving up, students with plans create strategies for overcoming obstacles when obstacles arise (and these strategies work!).

Does getting a job or starting a career seem light-years away? It's not. The future always arrives more quickly than we expect! Without help or planning, transitioning from high school to your preferred career can take years—even decades. Start work on this transition while you're still in high school, and you'll be in a good job by the time you're twenty-five. Your high school classes and extracurricular activities can build a strong base for your first career pathway.

Just like a savvy politician, you can use your high school years to set up a "campaign" that will help you achieve your future career goals. This campaign includes increasing your awareness of the work world, developing job-search skills, creating a career portfolio, and considering what kind of higher education will help you achieve your first career goals. We'll explore all of those things in this chapter.

And because it's good to think about what lies ahead, we'll also take a brief look at what comes after high school.

PARACHUTE TIP

In the United States, youth are eligible for hire with a work permit starting at age thirteen. If your high school has a work experience coordinator, go see this person to apply for a work permit.

AWARENESS OF THE WORK WORLD

There isn't a lack of jobs. In the United States right now, people work in 30,000 different jobs. In the 1980s, only 20,000 jobs existed. Regardless of what news media or politicians say, job options are growing, however slowly. Your challenge is to narrow down that list to a handful of job clusters that match your interests and strengths.

Remember that you always have options. Don't like your first choices? Pick another direction for your life and work. For example, your career goals may change as you learn that some technician-level jobs have salaries that exceed professional-level jobs. Don't mind a year or two of further study after high school but don't like the idea of four to six years? Check out technician jobs in fields or industries that interest you.

During your first two years in high school, learn the names of several dozen jobs in your favorite fields. In your remaining two years, study jobs in depth using the tools in this book. How well does each fit your parachute? All the work you've done in the preceding chapters—exploring your interests, skills, and preferences concerning work environments and identifying dream jobs—enlarges your awareness of the job market.

> In high school, I wish I'd known there were more options beyond doctor, lawyer, or businessperson. I also wish I'd known that you never have to choose what you are going to do forever. You can always change.
> —ALICE PRAGER, MARKETING MANAGER, AGE 29

Even without realizing it, you're probably already doing things that are helping your awareness to grow. You may, for example, be paying more attention to what people do to earn a living. You may take a career interest assessment that suggests some jobs you might like but didn't know about previously. You may have older friends or siblings who have left school and started jobs that you didn't even know existed. You may notice who enjoys their work and who doesn't. You may even start regularly asking adults what they do and how well they like it.

You can also help your awareness of the work world grow by using high school experiences—class assignments, extracurricular activities, part-time or summer work—to focus on your future.

Class Assignments

Need to do a book report? Read a book about a superstar in the industry that most interests you. Or choose a book on the basics of career development or some part of it that mystifies you. Your local bookseller will have lots of titles for you to consider.

Need to write a research paper? Pick a profession, field, or industry that fascinates you. For example, research Fortune 500 companies started by people with disabilities or who didn't finish college.

Just assigned a history report, and you love fashion? Report on the dress and fabric of a particular historical period.

Need to do an in-class presentation? Talk about what you learned in preparing your parachute and conducting your information interviews. In doing a presentation like this, you not only fulfill a class requirement but may also help your friends and classmates learn good skills for finding work they'll love.

Does your school have a community-service requirement for graduation? Look for ways in which you can serve your community and explore your career interests at the same time. Want to be a teacher? Volunteer at a learning-oriented nonprofit. Is politics your bag? Work with the Registrar of Voters to set up a program to register students who have turned eighteen.

Extracurricular Activities

Besides being fun and a great way to make friends, extracurricular activities can help you explore career possibilities and develop valuable skills. Band, choir, drama, tutoring, peer counseling, sports, service- or interest-based clubs, student government, and dozens of school activities can provide opportunities to test out interests and hone skills.

If you think you'd like to teach music, investigate creating your own summer business teaching music to younger students. Or perhaps your band or choir director will let you rehearse a new piece of music with the freshman choir or band. Exploring accounting? The responsibilities as treasurer of a club allow you to track income and expenditures, create a budget, collect dues, and so on. Serving as an officer of a club, a class, or the student body will help you develop both leadership and people skills, both of which can make you stand out to employers. Love drama? Write a play or musical about career-choice issues. Present it to parents or to elementary or middle school students.

PARACHUTE TIP

The "top skills" listed below are considered essential for college graduates to get good jobs in the twenty-first century. No matter what level of education you attain, your chances of getting a job are better if you have these skills. Pick classes, activities, or special programs that help you learn and practice these skills, and include examples of how you used these skills in your career portfolio.

Adaptability, flexibility

Analysis and synthesis of data

Communication: oral and written

Critical thinking

Drive, entrepreneurial mind-set

Global and multicultural awareness

Leadership, influencing others

Productivity, efficiency, accountability

Problem solving, decision making

Software, technical knowledge

Teamwork, collaboration

Time management: planning, organizing, prioritizing

Have a particularly supportive and encouraging teacher, club adviser, band or choir director, coach, or other faculty member in an extracurricular activity? Talk with them to find out how they can help you uncover jobs related to that activity and what skills you can develop now that would be valuable in that field.

Part-Time or Summer Work

Getting conflicting messages about whether or not you should work while you're in high school? Economist Steve Hamilton represents those who believe that teens should focus on their studies and get good grades. According to Dr. Hamilton, "Students get more long-term benefit from improving their grades than they do from a job at Arby's. Employers are looking for signals that a young person is motivated and ambitious. Grades are one signal." If you're a natural scholar or hoping for a merit or financial scholarship, this is particularly true.

But business owners believe that part-time or summer work during high school will help you develop important work-ethic, time-management, social, and job skills as well as a sense of responsibility. And in fact, GPA no longer makes top-ten lists of what employers want (although dip below 2.5 at your peril!).

REALITY CHECK

In this book, *college* is a synonym for any higher education or training after high school. When anyone says the word *college* to you, ask what they mean! Don't assume that you know.

Perhaps family finances even require that you work while in high school. Keep in mind that any job can be used to develop skills that can make you more employable down the line. Evaluate part-time jobs by what you can learn to make you more qualified for better jobs. Work in fast food? You gain valuable skills in working with the public. If you have a good supervisor, ask him or her to teach you some basic supervision skills. Interested in child development? A job at a child-care center will help you learn about that field. Can you get an entry-level job in a field that fascinates you? Through research and meeting people who work in that field, it could happen to you!

Here's some advice to etch in stone: save a third of your paycheck. No kidding. Teenagers typically spend 98 percent of what they earn. Spending beyond our means has gotten our country and its citizens into huge financial messes. Saving a few thousand dollars from high school jobs means you'll have money for necessary tools or lab fees, college textbooks, or a trip to check out a potential school, employer, or professional conference (where you can meet dozens of people who do the work that interests you).

Savvy Academic Choices

In high school, you have to meet certain academic requirements just to graduate, but you do have freedom to choose your electives. Making savvy academic choices now can help you land your dream job later on. Think you'll be going to college? Check with your college adviser or the catalog of a college that interests you. Schedule high school courses that will be most beneficial to you when you get to college. For example, certain AP (advanced placement), language, or technical courses may actually fulfill college requirements, enabling you to begin work on your major earlier and finish college sooner.

What if you're not certain about your future? Here are some ideas to help you no matter what you decide to do after high school:

• Keep your grades up. Strive to get the best grades you can. With each report card, ask yourself, "Did I do the best I could in every class?" If your answer isn't yes, up your effort.

• Is one of your goals in life to get a well-paying job? Take as many math and science classes as you can master. Challenging careers and high-paying jobs often rely heavily on math and science. If your school lacks good teachers in these areas, find a tutor, local class, or self-help math book. A librarian or knowledgeable bookstore salesperson can give you suggestions for books that are popular and easy to use.

REALITY CHECK

Fewer than half of those who start college finish their degrees. Check out other options for gaining the preparation necessary for the work you want to do.

• Language skills are very valuable. In addition to English, the languages of choice in the business world are Spanish and Mandarin Chinese. Want to work in a specific country? Challenge yourself to master that language while in high school. It's well known that the younger you are, the easier it is to learn a new language.

• Broaden your horizons. Learn more about your community, your country, and the world. Through your church or synagogue or temple, a community-service organization, or a nonprofit agency, you may be able to find volunteer projects in your home county or abroad.

• Talk to adults you know and respect. How did they come to do what they're doing? Find out what they like and don't like about their work. What tips do they have for you? What do they wish they'd known earlier?

DEVELOP JOB-SEARCH SKILLS

Get good at job hunting. You'll be using those skills often. The average millennial will have eighteen jobs in two or three fields. The ability to get a job in any market is a survival skill.

You've already started gaining job-search skills by doing the exercises in this book. We covered basic job-hunting techniques in chapter 4, and chapters 9 and 11 will introduce new techniques and explore the basics in greater detail.

Until you get your dream job, you'll need to keep honing your skills. Along the way, they may help you land an internship or a good part-time job or summer job while you're in high school. Luckily, as your skills develop, the job search will become easier, more efficient, and more effective—maybe even close to fun!

PARACHUTE TIP

The *Wow* factor. You've got it. Adults will be amazed that you aren't waiting until after you graduate to find your career fit. They will say, "Wow! I wish I'd done this at your age."

Job searching is a people-to-people experience. Go out and talk with employers in your city, town, or county who hire people to do work that interests you. If you want to live where you grew up, knowing local employers is an absolute necessity. If you are polite and prompt in your meetings or phone calls with adults, they will likely bend over backward to help you.

Here are a few activities to increase your awareness of jobs in fields that fascinate you and develop your job-search skills:

• Listen to guest speakers. Ask them, What first jobs did they get in their field? What do they look for in new hires? What classes should you take to put you on the right track?

• Explore jobs. Attend career days, visit friends or relatives in job settings, develop new contacts and conduct information interviews, get involved in volunteer work.

• Type the name of a job, field, or organization into the "Find friends" box on Facebook. You'll find people in your area and all around the country from whom you can learn more (always remember to use Internet safety precautions).

• Go to local conferences or meetings of professional organizations. Membership officers can tell you when the meetings are and if you can come as a guest. As a teen, you may be able to attend conferences for free. If you're shy about going to a professional meeting or conference on your own, attend with a parent, teacher, or other adult you trust. A friend can also come along for moral support; choose someone who will help you make a good first impression.

> Visited an In-and-Out Burger restaurant lately? Every member of the team is fully engaged and treats customers with courtesy. I'm hiring a kid that has those skills. I won't fret too much about their GPA.
>
> **–JIM ASCHWANDEN, RANCHER AND EXECUTIVE DIRECTOR, CALIFORNIA AGRICULTURAL TEACHERS' ASSOCIATION**

In all of your explorations, be respectful in your questions. Listen closely to answers. Ask for referrals. Send thank-you notes. You will receive lots of helpful suggestions from people you meet and contact.

Job Shadowing

Do you try on lots of outfits before choosing what to buy? Job shadowing lets you try on lots of jobs before you spend a dime on higher education.

Job shadowing is following a person doing a particular job for a day. You might shadow a business executive, a nurse, an architect, a teacher, or an actor. You can sit in on meetings or phone calls. Make contacts with clients or agents. Watch your host work at the computer or design table. Listen to how she teaches math to third-graders or prepares lines for a performance.

REALITY CHECK

Fear you'll be stuck with your very first job choice? Don't worry—the US work market is changing too fast to expect a first career to last throughout your work life. The US Bureau of Labor predicts that your generation will have an average of eighteen jobs in at least two career fields during a work life that will span fifty years. So you don't have to choose a career right now that will last a lifetime—just begin by figuring out your strongest interests and skills, and things will fall into place from there.

Job shadowing gives you a real feel for the day-to-day reality of specific jobs. Both job shadowing and on-site information interviews allow a first-hand experience of work environments to help you decide if they feel like a good fit for you.

Workplace visits show the job in 3-D and can be very compelling. Try not to make any learning or education commitments until you've seen at least three workplaces that interest you. Otherwise, how would you know whether you've shadowed someone whose job is not typical? You'll get a better idea of what "normal" is by shadowing multiple people.

Job shadowing can be either informal or formal. Informal shadowing might be done with a parent, boss, or someone you've interviewed for career information, and might last two to four hours. Enthusiastic about a job? Ask for a half day. Want more time? Additional time can be scheduled on another day at your host's convenience, or your host may have suggestions for someone else to shadow.

Formal job shadowing is usually set up through a school, career center, or other organization. Many businesses, schools, professional organizations, agencies, and institutions use Groundhog Day, February 2, to sponsor formal job shadowing. Start early: Halloween or Thanksgiving is a good time to start checking with your school to see what job-shadowing experiences will be available in your community as part of this national program. If no one in your school knows about this, call your local chamber of commerce. If you're good at organizing and want to show initiative, another option is to set up your own informal program or start a Job-Shadowing Club at your school.

Groundhog Day programs are a good introduction, but once a year isn't enough: good decision making requires good information. First-year students, try to schedule at least three job-shadowing events per year; sophomores, five; juniors, seven; and seniors, nine. Summers, when workplaces are often less formal, are a good time to pursue job shadowing.

In addition to giving a first-hand look at jobs that might match your parachute, job shadowing can uncover mentors. Mentors are so helpful, you may want more than one. Mentors can help you recognize and develop your most valuable skills in a particular field and give you guidance on the education or training you'll need. They can link you to contacts for summer employment in your field while you're going to school. They can help you land a full-time job when you're ready. Mentors can give you references for job hunting and continue to guide you on the job. A good mentor is invaluable; he or she will share experience, wisdom, insight, and practical knowledge that you won't learn in school. You can formally ask someone to be your mentor, or reach out to someone now and then when you need help. Every time your mentor spends time with you, be sure to follow up with a thank-you note.

PARACHUTE TIP

Tips from the tech sector:[3]

- Become great at Excel
- Learn to code
- Start reading faster
- Improve your public speaking skills
- Understand basic statistics
- Learn to negotiate

3 Summer Anne Burton, 24 Invaluable Skills to Learn for Free Online This Year (*Buzzfeed*, January 3, 2014), http://www.buzzfeed.com/summeranne/24-invaluable-skills-to-learn-for-free-online-this-year.

Internships

Why so much buzz about internships? Employers like to hire young adults who have had them—especially more than one. Why? Multiple internships show initiative and signal an applicant's ability to become productive as quickly as possible with the least training. Without several internships, many bachelor's-degree-holding grads in certain fields find it tough to get hired.

High school internships provide practical experience in a supervised setting. An internship might span weeks or months, depending on how long it takes to learn specific skills or procedures. Internships at the high school level are usually unpaid. There are summer programs that do provide salaries or stipends, but internships aren't about money. They're about learning valuable skills that will make you more employable or provide you with firsthand information that will help you make sound decisions about your career goals. If you do well, your internship can also gain you business contacts and employment references. Stay in touch with people you meet through internships—you may find someone who wants to hire you once you've gotten more education or training.

Your high school guidance counselor or career center may know about formal internship programs. Adult members of your school's booster club or local service clubs may also help you find an internship. Your local chamber of commerce may sponsor internships with local businesses, or they might help you set one up.

With the help of a parent, teacher, or school adviser, you can set up your own internship. Type "creating my own internship" into an Internet search box for more guidance. Identify a local business or agency where you'd like to work. Meet with the owner or the department manager and ask if she's willing to let you be an intern. An internship proposal should be in writing. It should list the skills to be learned, the duration of the internship, the days and hours you need to be present, and who will supervise you during your internship.

Employers think of internships as jobs, and you should, too. If you're lucky enough to get one, show up every day on time and willing to learn.

---------------------------- **EXPERT ADVICE** ----------------------------

THERE'S MORE TO INTERNSHIPS THAN A JOB OFFER
By Mark Babbitt, CEO of YouTern
www.linkedin.com/in/youternmark
mark@youtern.com

Despite the controversy over paid versus unpaid internships, many college students and recent graduates are completing several internships in order to gain that elusive first "real" job. However, according to many surveys, an internship results in a job offer less than 50 percent of the time.

So why are so many young careerists committed to internships? Here are five really good reasons.

A Degree Is Not Enough

Those students who still believe a high GPA and a degree will get them a job after graduation are living in denial.

In fact, according to a survey by the National Association of Colleges and Employers, nine out of ten direct-from-college hires have internship experience on their resumes. In the "2013 College Graduate Employment Study" by Accenture, more than 50 percent of employers feel college graduates need far more work experience to be seriously considered.

The one sure way of being perceived as employable: hands-on experience, through high-quality internships.

One Can Never Have Enough Mentors

Among those getting hired the soonest, there is another common factor: they have mentors. Many find their mentors within their chosen industry while completing an internship.

Career mentors are a special combination of adviser, sheriff, confidant, listener, and accountability partner. They keep you focused, shorten learning curves, and expand the thought process as new challenges are met. Perhaps most important: they help maintain the student's sanity while crossing the wide chasm between academic life and the real world through "been-there-done-that" wisdom.

Is Your Career Really the Right Choice?

College students work so hard to pick a compelling major and earn an attractive degree, but generally exert very little effort to make sure that the degree is the right one.

Nearly every day, we hear stories of accounting majors who, once they enter the field they spent four to six years in school to learn, truly dislike accounting. Or law school graduates who despise being attorneys. Or veterinary technicians who discover their jobs are not always about helping animals, but more about cleaning up the mess when something goes wrong. Internships not only verify our career choices; they help us avoid costly mistakes and correct our career paths.

Is Graduate School the Right Choice?

Perhaps more relevant: within your chosen career field, is graduate school even necessary?

Through 2012, 42 percent of recent grads felt they needed graduate school to compete well in the corporate world; they believed that a master's degree would make them more employable. Now, that number—according to a survey of 2013 graduates—has dropped to just 18 percent.

Why? Today's graduates are finding out that few really need graduate school, with the debt and loss of earning potential that come from pursuing an advanced degree. Their time is better spent developing mentor relationships, mastering good job-search skills, and building a strong personal network in order to learn directly from those already in the field.

Got Soft Skills?

Perhaps the most important reason to pursue internships while in college or immediately after graduation: soft skills. In a 2013 Jobvite survey, 41 percent of employers said that graduates without industry experience lacked the skills necessary to thrive in their first jobs out of college. The five skills most in demand:

• Written and oral communication skills (not academic style, but concisely written corporate communication)

• Problem solving (thinking about challenges and setbacks with a solution-oriented mind-set)

• Collaboration (both how well you work within the team and how well you lead when it's your turn to manage a project)

• Self-learning and coachability (your ability to absorb "just-in-time" lessons and meet new challenges as well as your ability to ask good questions, process the information provided, and adapt accordingly)

• Work ethic (millennials have a reputation when it comes to work ethic; for your own success, your job is to prove the stereotype wrong)

Internships don't guarantee a job offer. They do, however, create a foundation on which to build a successful early career. Complete at least one internship for each year of college . . . and jump well ahead of the job-search competition!

Career Portfolios

A career portfolio is a collection of information about you and the jobs that interest you. It's like your parachute, but with more details. Your portfolio can be as simple as a large envelope or a file folder in which you store all the information you've gathered. Career portfolios show proof of what you can do and what you know. They gather the information you need to apply for higher education, jobs, internships, special programs, or volunteer opportunities. This is the place to keep transcripts, letters of recommendation, a few strong samples of work you've done, newspaper articles about you or a team you played with, or paper copies of awards you've won. Learn to scan items into computer files, and keep those files and your hard copies organized and up-to-date.

You may create a career portfolio as part of a class. No such classes? If your high school has a career center, ask staff to help you. No center? Put together a career portfolio on your own. Do an Internet search using the phrases "creating a career portfolio" or "creating an eportfolio." If the advice seems too complicated, add the word "teen" to your search.

Have an interview for a college, job, or internship? Select the parts of your portfolio that best illustrate your skills and experience. Limit yourself to the top three examples of your work. Don't take your entire portfolio—your interviewer's eyes may glaze over.

Update your portfolio throughout high school and after. Keep the research already done. A contact you made or an interview you conducted could unexpectedly become important. Share parts of your career portfolio with adults who work in fields that fascinate you. Tell them your best skills and favorite interests. What fabulous jobs do they know about that you don't?

Develop a Three-Part Plan

"I'm going to college" is not a plan. It's a statement. It's an idea. It might not be a good idea. A one-choice plan is like a one-legged stool. It's going to let you down!

A three-part plan lets you compare options for your best post–high school learning plan. The My Favorite Interests section on the My Parachute diagram (page vii) lists three favorite fields. What is the one subject area or industry in which you would *most* like to work? Begin your three-part plan by answering the questions below (you may need to do some additional research):

• What entry-level jobs could I get in my favorite field (with or without a college degree) that would qualify me for better jobs in this field?

• What jobs could I get in my favorite field with two years (or less) of further training or education? What jobs could I qualify for with four years of technical training?

• With a bachelor's degree, what jobs could I do and like? What jobs would I qualify for with an advanced academic degree? Which of those interest me?

Once you accumulate this information, investigate a little further: What are costs for each option? How long will each take? What financial resources can you or your parents use? What amount could be borrowed, for how long, and at what interest rate? Research starting salaries for jobs you want. Will you earn enough for loan repayment? Gather all of the answers into a one-page chart for easy comparison. What choice gives you the most bang for your education buck?

By the start of your senior year, have your three-part plan completed and add it to your career portfolio. (Are you the particularly thorough type? Do a three-part plan for each of your favorite fields.) Using up-to-date research, your higher education planning won't be a dart game! Your three-part plan will help you design a successful strategy for what to do after high school.

SHOULD I GO TO COLLEGE?

The academic top 25 percent of any high school class can do well at college. Are you in that 25 percent? Students who know how their education relates to their future do especially well. Research shows that most young adults don't need a university degree right after high school. As a young adult, you need a way to support yourself through your twenties while you figure out your ultimate career goals.

Many adults believe that the longer you wait to make career decisions, the better your options. Ha! College grads with clear goals snap up good jobs months before graduation. Sophomores with career maturity already have

REALITY CHECK

- **By 15 years old:** Identify three fields that match your interests and find three jobs or clusters of jobs within each of those fields for further examination.

- **By 17 years old:** Know enough to select one field that most fascinates you and three jobs or a cluster of jobs within that field that fit you well.

- **By 18 years old:** Finish your parachute (chapters 1 to 4), create a three-part plan (see details on page 75), talk with enough people, and perform sufficient job shadowing or internships to choose your first career goal with confidence.

summer jobs or internships that get them needed work experience and add to their network of contacts. If you come out of college or university with over $30,000 in debt and no job prospects, life gets very stressful.

About one in three students enter and graduate from their university without having a clue what they are going to do with their education. The "wait and see what I fall into" game has been a great boon for coffeehouses seeking baristas. Just 33 percent of liberal arts graduates and 50 percent of grads from all majors get jobs that make use of their expensive educations. In 2013, 400,000 recent university grads worked fast-food front counters. Most gripe, "I got a degree for this?" Yes. Foolishly, they had no plan.

You can get a good job without graduating from college: only 21 percent of today's jobs require an academic degree. Will jobs of the future need more university graduates? The US Monthly Labor Review projects that by 2018, only 23 percent of jobs will require a bachelor's or higher degree.

> Libraries raised me. . . . I couldn't go to college so I spent three days a week for ten years educating myself in the public library, and it's better than college. People should educate themselves—you can get a complete education for no money.
>
> —RAY BRADBURY, AMERICAN AUTHOR, FILM PRODUCER, AND STORYTELLER

Many students leaving high school would be wise to start higher education at community colleges and technical institutes. In the four to six years it takes to get a bachelor's degree, technology may have already undergone two or three cycles of change. (Over 60 percent of students take six years to earn their bachelor's.) For many employers, the degree process is too slow. They constantly need workers with a good technical skill base who can quickly learn more skills. In some industries, one- or two-year technical degrees are more valued than bachelor's degrees. In 2014, 27 percent of those with some college out-earned the average bachelor's degree.

The Bureau of Labor Statistics predicts that today's teens will be in the workforce for fifty or sixty years. If you need a bachelor's degree for your ultimate career goal, you'll have plenty of time to acquire one. Serious question: Do you need one right away?

A university degree doesn't guarantee financial success. People are financially successful with and without them. A passionate interest may be a better indicator of financial success.

The late Srully Blotnick, a PhD in business psychology, wanted to know what happened to people who "go for the money." He studied the career choices and financial success of fifteen hundred MBAs. He divided them into two groups. Group A, 83 percent of the people in the study, chose careers they believed they could earn a lot of money doing. Group B, 17 percent of the study group, chose careers because of their interest in the work. Who do you think made more money?

Twenty years later, 101 of the fifteen hundred had become millionaires. One hundred of them were from Group B, who made choices based on interests. Only one millionaire was from Group A, who chose careers to make money. This research showed that *you are one hundred times more likely to be financially successful if you do work you enjoy.*

Nothing says you can't combine a university education and your passion. College can be a good place to develop and hone your fascinations and interests and enlarge your professional network. Of course, so is any job or activity in which you are currently involved. At university, college, or a technical institute, in the military or an apprenticeship, make time to make those connections.

> After working for a few months, I have a better understanding of what skills I need to advance in my field. I have been able to identify what I can learn now in order to make my job better in the future. I love how inexpensive and flexible community college is for this purpose.
> —MELANIE TOLOMEO, SALES AND MARKETING COORDINATOR, BLUE PLANET TRAINING

If you choose to go to work right out of high school, you can still go to college later—although if you decide to have a family of your own, that may present a new set of challenges, so you'll want to reflect on all the possibilities.

Think about a ladder. Each step takes you closer to the top. You can gain your education or training in steps, too. Work a while to build your skills and bank account, then go to school for a while. Repeat this cycle until you

REALITY CHECK

Twelve years of classes! The idea of more years of study doesn't thrill you? Unemployment is high among young adults—during the school year, it's 20 percent, or one out of every five students who wants to work. In the summer, it reaches 50 percent. A technical certificate or license might take only a few months to finish and can greatly boost your earning potential.

Can't face another day of school? Consider a "gap." You don't have to take a whole year—or you might take two. This gap isn't a vacation paid for by your parents. This is a focused time for work, volunteering, an internship, a few classes on subjects of strong interest, maybe some travel. Use the time to learn what you need to know to make better career plans.

achieve your ultimate career goal. For generations, this option for achieving education goals has been chosen by students who are ambitious but who lack ample financial resources.

You can see that there are numerous factors to consider when deciding whether or not, and when, to go to college. The answer isn't an easy yes or no. (As we go to press, this article from TheWeek.com, "Measuring the Value of College," provides the most balanced and accurate depiction of the factors: http://cdn.app.theweek.com/editions/com.dennis.theweek .issue.issue687/data/28364_4b4dba5ae91698afbc451ba77ebb60e7/web .html). It's important to remember that the choice you make today doesn't prevent you from making another choice later. Even if you feel you've made a wrong turn, you can choose another direction for your life and work.

Note: Some high school students have reported that teachers and counselors treat them like losers if they admit they're not interested in going to college to earn a bachelor's degree right after graduation (even if they're good students just planning a "gap year" to pursue other interests). This breaks our hearts and ticks us off. E-mail us at parachute4teens@gmail.com if this has happened to you.

DO I EVEN NEED TO GRADUATE
FROM HIGH SCHOOL?

If by age sixteen you're bored beyond belief with high school, head on over to your local community college and take the entrance exams. Pass them? Great. Consider enrolling. Many community colleges have programs that enable you to finish your high school diploma while taking college-level classes.

Can't pass the proficiency levels in math, science, or English? If you were to enroll in community college at this point, you would be put into remedial classes. The more remedial classes you have to take, the more likely you are to drop out—students who have to take just three remedial classes are 70 percent more likely to quit. Community college is your best and cheapest resource for education or training that will lead to good jobs, so you don't want to waste the opportunity. Best to stop your trash talk and redouble your efforts to learn in your high school classes.

A lot of so-called blue-collar trade jobs are now more highly paid than a lot of white-collar jobs. So, if we're talking about worthwhile jobs that are interesting, challenging, and well paid, then that sort of white-collar/blue-collar distinction is not a very good indication, any longer, of what goes on in the labor market.
—THE HONORABLE MICHAEL CULLEN,
NEW ZEALAND MINISTER OF HIGHER EDUCATION
AND FINANCE, 2007

HIGH SCHOOL: WHAT'S HAPPENING NOW

By Shawn Cowley, MBA, teacher and former soldier
www.linkedin.com/pub/shawn-cowley/0/55/38a

"You're joining the Army? Really? Why would you want to do that?" a high school classmate's mother condescendingly asked me back in 1984 in the spring of my senior year. I simply shrugged back then, but in hindsight, it was the wisest decision of my life.

First and foremost, I knew myself. I lacked the discipline and focus to steer away from the temptations of college at eighteen and avoid wasting thousands of dollars on an education without a clear objective. I recognized that I had no true career plan at that time. My high school wrestling coach, my father, the neighborhood parents—everyone greeted my decision with disappointment. My best friend said, "You would have been the ultimate frat boy!" "Exactly," I thought.

Only 50 percent of students who enter college actually graduate. A third of them drop out in their very first year. Yet still, in the school district that I work in, the overwhelming emphasis is placed on getting into college. Parents are doing a great job of taking students to visit college campuses, but they are not putting the same level of effort into exposing them to desired career fields.

Here's an example of why this is a problem. I've seen many students take an engaging and interesting psychology class in high school, then decide to pursue a career as a psychologist. Excited about the field, they go on to college and suddenly discover the rigor of the science classes required (side by side with pre-med students) and the necessity of a graduate degree, more school, more debt—all this with no clear path to becoming a practicing and employed psychologist. Discouraged, they quickly change majors or drop out.

The good news is that we are getting better. Many elective classes and extracurricular activities are implementing career exploration into their curricula. A few examples: Future Business Leaders of America, Project Lead the Way (an engineering-based program), Junior ROTC (a character/citizenship program), and Distributive Education Clubs of America. More young men and women are taking advantage of the Boy Scouts of America's Explorers program and other internship-based programs to provide real-life experience in their career fields of interest. Apprenticeship2000.com is a fantastic program that puts students in an actual job while attending community college—an apprenticeship program styled after those in Europe. Our school district has brought back vocational-based learning in magnet schools.

Programs like these can provide you with pathways and mentorships from high school through advanced education, leading the way to jobs in desired and growing career fields. Exploring these opportunities may help you make the best decisions of *your* life.

POSTSCRIPT: LIFE AFTER HIGH SCHOOL

Well-paying, interesting jobs require some amount of additional education or training. As we've discussed, you can continue higher education after you graduate from high school or wait a couple of years. Not ready for college or advanced technical training now? After a few years of work, going back to school may sound fun. Young adults returning to school after they've worked for several years often become great students. They have valuable work and life experience, and they are clear on what they want in life—so they go for it!

PARACHUTE TIP

Going to community college? Build a budget for three years. That's the average amount of time it takes young adults to complete a two-year degree. *Going to a state college or university?* Build your budget for five or six years. Only one out of three students finishes his bachelor's in four years.

What do *you* want to do after high school? Imagine you and your friends are brainstorming about the future. What ideas might you hear? What ideas would you contribute? Here are a few:

• Travel—around the country or around the world.

• Take a gap year. No matter what you do or where you go, use your time to create plans for your first career path.

• Get a part-time or full-time job and continue your education (go to a two-year or four-year school, take online courses, get a technical certificate or license, or learn a skill or trade).

• Get a part-time job and do volunteer work to learn more skills and to make contacts that will help you in your job search.

• Get any job in your favorite field or industry to learn more about it.

• Figure out a job that could be in demand anywhere in the world. Get qualifications. Go.

• Check out a new city or state (or even country!) to live in.

• Look into studying abroad.

• Begin a government apprenticeship.

• Create your own apprenticeship.

• Get a fun job, even if it's not what you want for a career.

• Join the Peace Corps, State Civilian Conservation Corps, Job Corps, or AmeriCorps. Information about these organizations is available on the Web.

• Join the military.

Getting ideas? Look at the drawing on the next page. More ideas swirling? Add them to the list. What are your top three choices? Whatever you choose to do, do it with your whole heart. Live your life to the fullest. Your twenties are an important time to establish a good foundation for your work or career. They should also be fun.

CHAPTER 6

WHAT DO I DO NEXT?
make the most of the best and least expensive higher education

> Where you go after high school—whether you go to college and which college you go to—is much less important than *what* you study.
>
> —RICH FELLER, PHD, PROFESSOR AND AUTHOR OF *KNOWLEDGE NOMADS AND THE NERVOUSLY EMPLOYED*

Going to college? Great! The Discovery Exercises in part 1 give you a big advantage over other students beginning college. Have you completed them? If so, you know what's important to you and what you need to study to find work you'll love. Over half the students who start college drop out. Many who quit say they had no idea why they were in college and were not fully committed to completing their education. Career focus gives you that strong commitment.

In the '60s, '70s, and into the '80s, young adults went to college to discover what they wanted to do. Most found good jobs after graduation simply because they had a college degree. You do not live in that world. In your world a college degree doesn't guarantee either employment or high pay. Since 2009, college graduates have entered a very rough job market. These economic conditions are expected to continue. Currently, just half of recent grads with bachelor's degrees have found work that requires their level of education. This is not intended to discourage you from going to college if you need a bachelor's degree for the work you want to do. It is meant to underscore that you must juggle academics and career development. Your studies are no excuse to ignore the labor market where you want to live, your career goals, or expanding your contacts while in school. Don't treat your college education like a very expensive lottery ticket: tens of thousands of dollars spent for the chance at a good job.

CHECKLIST: GETTING THE MOST OUT OF COLLEGE

☐ Get the most from your higher education while you learn the skills employers want.

☐ Learn how to prioritize and manage your time well. For the rest of your life, you'll have competing priorities. Knowing how to perform well while juggling multiple tasks is a skill you need.

☐ Go to office hours in the first week. Introduce yourself before your professors get too busy so you will stand out.

☐ Take classes outside your comfort zone. These expand your worldview and your creativity.

☐ Find the best professors you can. Don't ignore the 8:00 a.m. class taught by a terrific professor. Whether in your major or an elective, you get more bang for your education buck from classes with good teachers.

☐ Take classes that will help you in life and work in real-world situations. Consider leadership development, foreign language, business communications, or entrepreneurship.

☐ Don't be intimidated by small seminar classes. You can learn exponentially more than in those huge, anonymous, lecture-hall survey classes.

☐ Find your college's learning resource center. What resources do they have to help you learn effective study skills? Unless you got a perfect SAT (2400) or ACT (36) score, you'll probably need to amp up your study skills from high school level.

☐ Learn to think critically, which includes recognizing and filtering out unnecessary information.

☐ Select a few extracurricular activities and take on a leadership role. Pick one that's a deep interest you'll want to do for several years; others can be short term. If one of them is an exercise routine, your mind and body will thank you.

☐ Acquire social skills and build friendships. The ability to do both will enrich your personal and professional lives.

☐ Get to know your alumni network—soon. Don't wait until graduation. Find out when your department will hold its next alumni event. Go and practice your social skills while building contacts. Alums can answer field-related questions and give you tips on good professors, internships, summer jobs, or permanent ones.

☐ Plan for multiple internships or a part-time job to immerse you in the realities of the jobs you think you want.

CONTINUED

INVEST IN YOURSELF

Investment is defined as the process of putting money into something in the anticipation of profit or a material result. Higher education is a classic investment; the money invested now will make more money later. The biggest threat to your college education is using up all your financial resources on your first degree. The second biggest threat to your investment is not taking advantage of your time in college to improve your employability. The third biggest threat? Dropping out with debt and no improved employability.

Your college years can be very rich and rewarding in many ways, but they also require a new sense of responsibility for your personal life and for your financial life. Your college education is an investment in your future. It's up to you to make it pay off.

PARACHUTE TIP

The best get-the-most-out-of-college book is Suzette Tyler's *Been There, Should Have Done That: 995 Tips for Making the Most of College*. Make your parents read it with you. They will groan over all the opportunities they didn't know about and missed!

FINANCIAL REALITIES OF COLLEGE AND ACADEMIC DEGREES

It may seem odd to bring up the topic of finances so early in this chapter, but the financial realities of college affect your life not only while you're in college but also—if you borrowed money through student loans or accumulated credit card debt—for years afterward. If your parents are paying for part or all of your education, this affects their lives and possibly their ability to retire.

Your teachers may tell you that you must get a college degree "no matter what it costs." Some folks may tell you that all student loan debt is good debt. Don't listen. These well-meaning people won't be the ones paying off *your* student loans. Carrying five to ten thousand dollars of debt is hard. The adults around you should know this if they remember paying off their first car loan or their own student loans.

> A designer degree doesn't matter nearly as much in the long run as the things a student does while getting that piece of paper— especially the activities and jobs between classes and during the summer. Those are the things that will truly contribute to a depth of self-discovery, transforming college students into adults with not only education but confidence, job skills, and a global perspective, too.
> —HOLLY ROBINSON, AUTHOR AND BLOGGER

Almost all private student loans are bad debt. Unless there is no alternative and you need to borrow only a small amount, avoid private student loans. They are not regulated by the government and don't qualify for federal repayment programs. Private loans have no reasonable cap on the interest (rates can go up to 23 percent) or the fees you can be charged.

Research starting salaries for the jobs you want. Salaries for experienced workers are important for career decision making, too. Big caution: It's your starting salary that determines how much you can afford to borrow for your degree or training. Once you know the likely starting salaries for jobs that interest you, take that number, divide it by three, and multiply it by two. The resulting number is the total amount you can afford to borrow.

It's a mistake to assume that all academic degrees translate into increased earnings when you join the workforce—they don't. The highest-paying major's average starting salary is $63,000 more than the lowest-paying major's. Make no assumptions about the pay of the jobs you want—check out possible starting salaries on www.glassdoor.com/salaries. Since salaries vary widely throughout the country, check with employers where you want to live, too.

THE UNEQUAL EARNING POWER
OF COMMON MAJORS[4]

- Petroleum engineering: $96,200
- Computer engineering: $70,300
- Chemical engineering: $66,900
- Computer science: $64,100
- Aerospace/aeronautical/astronautical engineering: $63,900
- Mechanical engineering: $63,900
- Electrical engineering: $62,500
- Engineering technology: $62,500
- Management information systems: $60,300
- Logistics/materials management: $59,500
- Management of companies/enterprises: $57,500
- Finance: $57,400
- Marketing: $51,000
- Communications: $43,700
- Accounting: $43,000
- Information systems: $43,000
- History: $41,900
- English: $40,200
- Sociology: $37,000
- Social work: $36,000
- Criminal justice $34,800
- Visual and performing arts: $33,800
- Psychology: $33,500

4 Average starting salaries from the National Association of Colleges and Employers, 2012/2013.

Let's say that you and your college roommate pay the same tuition, $117,500 total. Completing your degrees takes each of you five years at a cost of $23,500 per year. You each borrow $33,000 in student loans. Your roommate graduates with a degree in computer science. She accepts a job with a starting salary of $59,700. Your degree is in exercise physiology. Starting salaries average $32,500. The best job offer you've gotten so far is for twenty-six hours a week at $15.35 an hour. You hope to pick up another part-time job and cobble together an annual salary of about $30,000 a year.

How does your financial situation compare with that of your roommate? If your first job pays half what your roommate earns, your roommate's student loans will be paid off long before yours will. That $33,000 can double in less than ten years through charges for late or missed payments. If you want to pay off your student loan in ten years, your payment at 2 percent interest will be $304 per month. How will that affect where you live, what car you drive, and what you can afford to do in your free time?

Living on noodles is something many college students do. But as a twenty-something, watching friends party at a good restaurant while you can barely afford a microwave meal is very disheartening (not to mention of dubious nutritional value). For young adults whose dream jobs pay less than $35,000 a year and who would need to borrow more than $24,000 to gain their desired degree, work and education ladders are an excellent option (see page 78). Ladders allow you to get the educational qualifications you need without becoming an indentured servant to student loans.

> Don't take on too much debt. Most students would be smart to limit their total borrowing to no more than two-thirds of the annual salary they expect to make in their first year after college. If you're at or near that limit and haven't finished your schooling, consider transferring to a cheaper college or taking a year off to work and pay down your loans.
> —LIZ PULLIAM WESTON, MSN MONEY CENTRAL

Higher education debt is a major issue for college students, their parents, and their grandparents. Seniors are having social-security checks garnished to pay off old student loans! About a third of college graduates leave school in serious financial difficulty. According to college officials, more students drop out of college due to debt than due to bad grades. College students who don't take the time to do careful financial planning, make career contacts, and select job targets before graduation are extremely vulnerable.

With the current financial realities of college in mind, how can you make the most out of your college years, particularly in terms of finding work you'll love? Continue to increase your awareness of jobs in your favorite fields or industries. Hone your job-search skills. The difference from high school is that you'll do these things with more depth, enthusiasm, and focus, since you'll be much closer to the day when you'll need to go out and use your skills to land a good job.

> The way we have funded higher education in this country has had the unintended consequence of indenturing an entire generation of students who now comprise the "educated poor."
> —ROBERT APPLEBAUM, LAWYER AND FOUNDER OF FORGIVESTUDENTLOANDEBT.COM

REALITY CHECK

- 70 percent of recent graduating college seniors had student loans. The average amount borrowed was $32,500. That debt was made up of (1) student loans, (2) personal or family loans, and (3) credit card charges. Grads with this much debt need annual starting salaries of at least $48,750 to be able to live and pay their bills.

- 50 percent of college grads were surprised by how much debt they had accumulated.

- 30 percent of recent college grads had no debt. Try to be one of them![5]

5 Accenture 2014 College Graduate Employment Survey

TOP TEN FINANCIAL CONCEPTS FOR TEENS

By Chris Shannon, youth advocate and educator
www.linkedin.com/in/chrisshannon1

I counsel teens on finances and careers because this was information I never received, and if I had, my life would be so different.
When asked, "What are some of the most important lessons a teen
can learn about money?" I came up with the following list. I hope it
helps you as you move toward your own independent life!

Define what being "rich" or "wealthy" means to you.

People always believe that things would be better if they were rich,
but no one ever defines *rich*. Does it mean owning a fully paid-off
home? Providing for a family? Traveling? Owning nice things? Wealth
isn't a dollar figure; it's a state of mind. A millionaire could still consider himself "struggling" whereas someone living in poverty could
have everything she needs. What is that state of mind for you?

Make a plan for your money.

"If you don't have a plan for your money, someone else does,"
says Leo Macneil, senior vice president of community relations at
HarborOne Credit Union. There are tons of free budgeting materials
and apps available online; shop around until you find one that works
for you. Document all of your income as well as expenses. Identify
your spending preferences and values. Would you rather pay for
good food or good clothes? Sports or a concert? Once you create
a realistic budget, track your spending and adjust as necessary to
meet smart goals for your money.

**Realize that your spending choices are influenced by your friends
and the media.**

There's a reason they call advertising "the fine art of separating
people from their money." Celebrities and advertising help us define
what we think will make us attractive, accepted, strong, smart, or
successful. Even stores arrange what they sell in a way to influence
what you buy—ever go in for "one thing" and come out with a lot
more than you planned? The more aware you are of outside influ-
ences on your spending choices, the more control you have over
spending your money the way *you* want.

Figure out ways to maintain a positive cash flow.

Plan to have more money coming in than going out. Make your money work for you, such as earning interest in a savings account.

> People need to approach college like they approach purchasing a car. Different people can afford different models. Don't be deterred from going to college, but students need to be smart shoppers.
>
> —ANYA KAMENETZ, JOURNALIST AND AUTHOR OF *GENERATION DEBT* AND *DIY-U*
> (If you're going to college or considering it, read both books!)

A bad financial reputation could cost you!

A good credit score could save you a *lot* of money in what you pay to borrow—people with good credit scores are charged lower interest rates on large purchases, such as a house or car, and on credit cards. Of course, there are other benefits, such as a better chance of landing that job or renting that apartment.

Realize there is a *cost* to borrowing money.

Credit is a *business*—companies are in it to make money from you. Use it wisely. Understand the contract you sign when you get a loan or apply for a credit card, and know the fees and interest rates up front.

Invest in yourself.

Take advantage of opportunities to enrich yourself through knowledge and experience, and you will increase your "human capital"—your worth to potential employers. Make lifelong learning a habit. The more you know, the more you can do, the more you are investing in yourself—your one greatest asset!

It's not just about the salary.

When listing the factors that influence job satisfaction, salary is not first. Or second. Or even third. You don't realize the value of certain job benefits until you need them. Do they pay for health insurance? Provide paid time off? Help finance education or healthy living choices? All of these have a financial impact on you. But other benefits might be a better match for your values and lifestyle. Can you get paid to travel? Will they allow time off for volunteering? Do they provide day care or have a gym on-site? Consider the value of the big picture. Then decide if a job opportunity is a match for *you* and not just your wallet.

Shop around.

You are in control of who handles your money and who earns money from lending to you or protecting you. Comparison shopping is a great idea not just for the large and small purchases you make but for the companies you will trust with your money, your identity, your safety, and your future—for instance, banks, credit card companies, and insurance companies.

Watch your back . . . and your passwords, your cards, your photo ID . . .

Take steps to minimize fraud and identity theft. Don't loan out cards, give friends PIN numbers, or order things online in public places. Be careful of when, where, and to whom you give out your social security number, address, e-mail, or birth date. This is one time when it can pay to be paranoid.

PARACHUTE TIP

Personal savings plans run from the extremely simple ($52 saved at $1 a week; $1040 saved at $20 per week) to the extremely complex, using percentages of income. Try the "52 Week Money Challenge" that was circulating on Facebook a while back: week 1, save $1. Week 2, save $2, and so on. By the end of the year you'll have saved $1,387!

CULTIVATE QUALITIES, DEVELOP SKILLS

As you select your classes, major, and extracurricular activities, keep in mind what employers look for in new hires. Plan your courses, extracurricular activities, internships, or volunteer work so that you are proficient in the qualities and skills employers want. Anyone hoping to get hired in the field of her dreams should be able to demonstrate and provide examples of these skills.

In college and on the job, success means showing up 99 percent of the time. One quality employers demand is a strong work ethic. This means that you're willing to work hard; you're dependable, responsible, and punctual; you take seriously the work you do for your employer; and you do that work as well as you possibly can. According to the National Association of Colleges and Employers' Job Outlook 2014 survey, the top skills that employers are looking for are "ability to work in a team structure," "ability to make decisions and solve problems," and "ability to plan, organize, and prioritize work."[6]

Information interviews and job shadowing let you observe work ethics in operation at each place of business. Behavior encouraged by one employer may not be expected—or tolerated—by another. You need to find a good fit between your own work ethic and that of your employer. When you have a job interview, *you* are actually interviewing the *employer* as much as the employer is interviewing you.

> Shut off your cell phones, cover your body, turn off the video poker, unplug your iPod, stop text messaging your friends, and get to work.
> —YOUNG SILICON VALLEY EXECUTIVE TO RECENT COLLEGE GRADS

PARACHUTE TIP

Being a team builder, good listener, and great communicator will make you a good employee. Want to be a CEO? Different traits are preferred. Executive and organizational skills are most important. The traits that lead to executive success are attention to detail, persistence, efficiency, analytic thoroughness, and the ability to work long hours.

---

6 National Association of Colleges and Employers, Job Outlook: The Candidate Skills/Qualities Employers Want, (*Job Outlook 2014*, October 2, 2013), http://www.naceweb.org/s10022013/job-outlook-skills-quality.aspx.

REALITY CHECK

New on the job? Work in a large corporation? Look at your work clothes. Are they appropriate? If you don't know, check out what the bosses are wearing. If you consistently offend a long-time employee with your work attire, chances are you will be let go and never be told that was the reason why.

CONTACTS

In addition to developing the qualities and skills that employers want most, it's important to use your college years to gain work experience and develop relationships with your professors and supervisors. Information interviews, job shadowing, internships, part-time jobs, or summer jobs are good ways to expand the range of people you know. Keep a list of whom you meet, their contact information, and how you met them.

Information Interviews and Job Shadowing

Continue doing information interviews as you did in high school, but now do them in more depth. (To review information interviewing and job-shadowing techniques, see chapters 4, 5, 9, and 10.) Ask to meet with people for thirty minutes, and request more detail about the day-to-day realities of their jobs and the direction they see their career field taking—including what opportunities or obstacles that might present for you.

Chapter 5 offered some basic information about job shadowing. You can use the same technique in college to learn more about particular jobs. With additional life, academic, and work experience, you'll now ask better questions and get better information as a result.

Can your college career center help find people (perhaps alumni) for you to job shadow or interview? Faculty members in the area of your major, as well as your college roommates and friends (and their parents), may also provide important contacts. Get in touch with your college's office of alumni relations. Good schools have databases about their grads that include employment information. Read one or two professional journals regularly. Get in touch with the authors of articles that interest you. (If you find you have no interest in reading a professional journal, how can you contemplate working in that field?)

Don't forget those people you job shadowed or did information interviews with when you were in high school. If your interests still lie in the same area, consider contacting them again for suggestions or opportunities.

Internships

Internships are designed to introduce you to working in a particular field or job and to give you practical work experience. Employers prefer to hire college students who have done multiple internships. They weigh internship experience higher than grades, the college you attended, and even your professional recommendations. Ninety-one percent of employers don't care where you went to school. They want you to be able to do what they need you to do.

Check with the career center at your college for information on internships. Many companies and businesses offer internships to college students. Some are paid and some are not; some take place during the summer, others during the school year. Professional associations are a good source for internship leads as well. Want to be a vintner? The vintner's association in the region where you want to live may know of opportunities.

If you're unable to find an internship that fits your particular needs, try contacting several companies that you'd like to work for. Can you set up an internship with one of them?

The quality of internships varies wildly; some students report being active members of a team, while others say they just warmed a chair. Find students who have done internships that interest you. Interview them. Avoid internships that are a waste of time. Make sure you do your part: show up on time, professionally dressed and open to new assignments. If your experience is a good one, after you graduate you may be offered a full-time position at the business where you interned. (Don't be disappointed if that offer doesn't happen. Of the 72 percent of recent college grads who had internships, only 42 percent were offered jobs.) In addition to gaining new skills and greater confidence in yourself, if you impressed the people you worked with, they may offer to write professional references for you or connect you with potential employers.

PARACHUTE TIP

When you finish a class in which you did particularly good work, an internship, a volunteer project, or a job at which you have been complimented for your contributions, ask for a letter of recommendation before you leave. Even if your supervisor or professor likes and remembers you, he or she may have trouble remembering the details of your work after a few months. Get it in writing!

PARACHUTE TIP

Successful artists and creative types often go for internships in their teens. Montana-born Brad Bird, director of *The Incredibles*, was a Disney apprentice at fifteen years old. The successful freelance writer Anya Kamenetz was fifteen when she had her first newspaper internship. After high school, Anya continued to find internships and get jobs at magazines to sharpen her skills. In a dozen years, she became successful and well paid. Learn the steps Anya used by reading about her online.

YOU AS A BUSINESS

Young adults are referred to as "start-up adults." It's an interesting metaphor, as it alludes to a person in the first phase of business, just starting up. It's also a helpful metaphor. No business would spend $80,000 to $150,000+ (the cost of a bachelor's degree) on a new piece of equipment or a service without knowing what it would do for them. Smart college-goers won't either. The goal of your business plan is to leave college with a job you'll like and one that needs your college education.

ARE YOU BACKABLE?

Venture capitalists look for new businesses (called start-ups) that are likely to succeed.

Explore and increase your backability with these two books:

- *Backing U! Lite: A Quick Read Guide to Backing Your Passion and Achieving Career Success* by Vaughn Evans (Business and Careers Press, 2009)
- *Me 2.0:4 Steps to Building Your Future, Revised and Updated Edition* by Dan Schawbel (Kaplan Trade, 2011)

Want to be backable, like a start-up business that's irresistible to investors? Follow this timeline.

Summer of freshman year (or earlier): Complete your parachute and do enough information interviews to learn about three fields or industries that interest you. Find out what internships are available through your university.

Keep a list of names and contact information of all the people you meet who work in the field you also want to work in. Reading a few professional journals may help you make a choice among fields.

Sophomore year: Use breaks to investigate those careers further. You want to know which field or industry appeals to you most so that you can declare a major by the start of your junior year. (At academic universities, two out of every ten sophomores drop out before their junior year because they don't know what major they want to pursue.) Students who don't have a clue what they want to do with their major, or who change majors more than once, are more likely to get jobs that don't use their college degree. Apply for summer internships.

Summer of sophomore year: Get an entry-level job or internship in the industry that interests you most, or set up a series of volunteer internships in several fields so you can check them out. Update your contact list and your plan for success.

Junior year: Apply for summer internships abroad or for a term abroad. Employers want graduates who are global citizens. Find professional conferences or local professional association meetings to attend.

Summer of junior year: Secure an internship or job in your field. Identify the top five employers for whom you want to work. Find contacts at those organizations. Update your contact list and your plan for success.

Senior year: Organize your classes so that you can do another internship before you graduate. Keep learning about potential employers, and add another five to ten to your list. Get in touch with all of your contacts to let them know you are actively looking for work. Ask if they have any contacts at your preferred employers or have heard of any openings. If no openings come up, reach out to hiring managers and introduce yourself to set up a meeting. This is a sales meeting—you sell yourself as a qualified potential employee. While there still may be no job open, you might get referrals to some that are. (Seniors who graduate with a job lined up report that it took six to nine months of active job searching to secure it.)

> Your choices *in* college matter more than your choices *of* college.
>
> —PETER D. FEAVER, SUE WASIOLEK, AND ANNE CROSSMAN, AUTHORS OF *GETTING THE BEST OUT OF COLLEGE*

DECISIONS, DECISIONS

Before making a final decision on whether to go to college or which colleges are the best match for you, you'll need to consider, research, and evaluate the following issues:

Liberal arts or career-track major; private or public university; community college or university; double major or major and minor; living at home or on campus; taking a gap or going to university right after high school. And let's not forget: The quality of career centers, resources to overcome learning disabilities, campus safety, residential-life programs, and counselors to help with long- or short-term personal issues.

THE COLLEGE EXPERIENCE

Though our focus in this book is on helping you find work you'll love, life is more than just work. The college experience, in addition to providing you with academic grounding, also challenges you to discover what you truly value. You may get involved in sports, volunteer work, clubs, or other activities that you'll continue for decades. Routines started in college can help you balance the many different aspects of your life. Challenges and responsibilities that you didn't have to worry about very much while you were living at home in high school will help you grow and mature. Problems may include learning to work out differences with roommates, facing new

PARACHUTE TIP

Having trouble with study skills or understanding academic content? Ask for help! Find your college learning resource center. Utilize department assistants or tutors if you need them. If you're having difficulty with a particular class, talk with the professor or teaching assistant. Don't wait—do this as soon as you feel like you are floundering. Your initiative in getting help indicates a strong work ethic and a drive toward success.

REALITY CHECK

Seventy percent of the young adults who enter college intending to go on to graduate school never actually do. The problem? Many of them chose majors that don't have good prospects in the job market without that graduate degree. If you have the expectation of going to graduate school, try taking the entrance exam for the graduate study field of your choice during your senior year in high school. Regardless of your score, your reaction to this test will tell you a great deal about the odds of your being one of the 30 percent of bachelor's degree holders who are admitted to graduate studies.

financial realities, balancing study time with social time and work obligations, and maintaining an apartment (cleaning, grocery shopping, laundry, and cooking). If you ignore the challenges of college life and just party for four or five years, you'll waste not only a lot of money but also your opportunity to be better prepared for finding good, satisfying work after college. College is not the end of your career development. It's one way to qualify for work you'll love.

No time in life is quite like your college years. Have fun, learn as much as you can, and continue building a strong foundation for your future.

CHAPTER 7

GOAL SETTING
keep yourself motivated and move forward

> A goal is a dream with a deadline.
> —NAPOLEON HILL, AUTHOR OF THE CLASSIC BOOK
> *THINK AND GROW RICH*, 1937

As you've been reading the previous chapters, completing the exercises, and answering questions, you've been gathering information on your interests, skills, and potential dream jobs. This research has helped you discover your likes, dislikes, and hopes. You've read about using high school and college experiences to enhance your awareness of the work world and job readiness. Has this exploration given you ideas about how your interests give shape to potential work and your future? Goal setting is a tool that will help you do both.

A goal is something you want to achieve or accomplish: learning to drive a car, getting a high school or college diploma, or representing your school in a competition. A goal can be a desire to experience something you've wished for: traveling to India, going white-water rafting, or meeting a relative you've only heard about. Your goals may be personal: improving social skills, reading a particular book, or learning to get along with your little sister. Others may be academic: being admitted into college, earning a 3.0 GPA, or surviving chemistry. Some are work related: finding your dream job or getting an apprenticeship. Because life is about more than just school or work, your goals can relate to anything—relationships, learning, or just simply having fun.

Goals help us in many ways. Have you ever set a goal and achieved it? What did you learn about achieving a goal through this experience? Have you set a goal and *not* achieved it? Run through the experience in your mind. What got in your way that's in your power to change? What did you learn in the attempt? Failure, well studied, is a great teacher.

Goals help articulate (meaning "name and talk about") what we want to accomplish. They define what's most important to do with our time or how we must spend our time differently to achieve a goal. Goals also help motivate us to do what we say we want to do. The act of writing goals down makes them more real. Just saying we want to do something *someday* is not enough, since "something" and "someday" are ill defined, and rarely are unclear goals achieved. Change vagueness to clear, written-out goals. "In May of this year, I will jog a mile and not die or puke." You've articulated a feat you want to accomplish and given it a deadline.

Knowing your goals and setting milestones and deadlines to achieve them keeps you moving toward making them happen. A goal on a list is just an idea unless you put in effort to achieve it. When you achieve your goals, you feel better about yourself. Goal setting lets you discover and define how you'd like to spend your time, present and future. Life becomes more interesting, and you'll feel more in control of your destiny.

GOAL TIMELINES

Goals have different timelines and different pacing. Submitting an entry for a competition two weeks from now is paced faster than spending the summer teaching your cousins to swim. You may want to set three-month, six-month, or academic-term goals. Have papers to write or projects due? Listing what you must do day by day, week by week, or month by month will help you achieve your goals without stomach-turning, last-minute drama.

Identifying long-term goals takes more time and thought. Goals reflect values. When mulling over long-term goals, you need to know

• What is important to me?

• What do I most want to do with my time on earth?

These are not easy questions, but they are important to ponder. Some goals may change over time while others become clearer. Some show themselves unworthy of your time. Accomplish a goal? Set another one.

> A goal is not always meant to be reached;
> it often serves simply as something to aim at.
> —BRUCE LEE, MARTIAL ARTIST AND ACTOR

GOAL SETTING

Take a sheet of paper. Turn it so the long edge is horizontal, and fold it into four equal vertical columns. Draw a line near the top to create one row for column headings. Title the first column "What I hope to do in my life"; the next column, "Things I hope to do in the next one to three years"; the third column, "People have told me I should . . ."; and the last column, "If I were to die in six months, how would I want to spend my time?"

Set a timer for two minutes (or have a friend time you). Start with any column. Write down anything that comes into your head during those two minutes. After two minutes are up, set the timer for another two minutes and turn to one of the other columns. It makes no difference which one you do next. Complete all four columns. This whole exercise will take you just eight minutes.

Once you're done, read over each column. What are your reactions to what you've written? Are there surprises? Were any sections more difficult to complete than others?

Take a look at that last column, "If I were to die in six months, how would I want to spend my time?" What activities did you list? The activities you'd choose if you had little time to live would be those things you value most. Look at your list in that column. Does it reflect what is most important to you?

You probably have things you have to get done in six months or face serious consequences (term papers and finals). But life needs fun, too. What are some personal goals you'd like to accomplish or get started on in the next six months? If you've gained new perspective on your six-month goals, revise the list to reflect your actual goals for the next six months, both personal and those related to school or career planning.

Before prioritizing your goals, let a few days pass. Identifying what you want to do and experience in your lifetime may stimulate other ideas. Add each of these ideas to the appropriate column, depending on the time frame of the goal. When your list feels complete, prioritize the list so that the items first on your list are the most important to you. Write two or three favorite goals from each list at the center of your My Parachute diagram (page vii).

When your friends complain, "I didn't get much done this summer; I don't know where the time went," you'll know exactly where your time went—and you'll have a list of accomplishments to show for it.

ACCOMPLISH YOUR GOALS

A goal without a timeline is a wish. When you know your goals, it's important to plan how to accomplish them. Use a simple to-do list or an alarm on your smartphone, or note on a calendar the dates by which you want them finished.

Let's say that one of your goals is to attend a particular college or art or technical school. For each school, your to-do list might look like this:

1. Check school's website for admissions and application information and deadlines.

2. Visit www.university.linkedin.com/. Get the skinny on college applications and the institution itself.

3. Register to take the SAT (or other admissions tests).

4. Talk to a college admissions counselor about high school courses to take.

5. Register for those courses.

6. Take the SAT.

7. Fill out FAFSA (the Federal Student Aid Form; https://fafsa.ed.gov/).

Perhaps, while working your way through your to-do list, you discover that you don't have to take the SAT, but you must prepare a portfolio for admissions. Your revised to-do list might look like this:

1. Visit www.university.linkedin.com/. Get the skinny on college applications and the institution itself.

2. Get explicit requirements for the portfolio.

3. Talk with an admissions counselor about portfolio requirements or high school courses to take.

4. Begin assembling my portfolio.

5. Complete my portfolio by the application deadline.

6. Fill out FAFSA.

A to-do list breaks down your goal into manageable steps. If you make the steps too big, you may get discouraged. If the steps are just the right size, you'll keep moving toward your goal. If you find yourself avoiding your to-do list, that could be a sign you don't really want to achieve this goal, or the steps are too big. Break down the step that has you stuck into two or three smaller steps. Each time you complete a step, check it off. Completing a step is an accomplishment in itself. Each step you complete moves you closer to your goal.

REEVALUATE GOALS OFTEN

As you move toward a goal—particularly long-term goals—you'll have new experiences and gather new information that will help you evaluate that goal. What you learn moving toward a goal can be more valuable than achieving that goal. You may confirm that a particular goal is the right one for you, or revise it to include new ideas or new life directions. It's okay to let go of goals that no longer have meaning for you. Replace old goals with new ones that are more important to you.

PLAN BACKWARD

At a recent community talk on career choice for teens and young adults, a parent made this remark: "So, it seems that what you are saying is that career development happens backward. If we want to make good choices about higher education, we should first find out what employers we want to work for, meet them and ask them what course of study they recommend,

> In advising hundreds of Hispanic students—a vibrant community with exploding demographics and a group that has traditionally underachieved in the educational system—I have found that it is important for teens to develop a future orientation. Students must understand what it means to get from here to there. If a student in junior high school wants to become a physician, it is worth knowing the important milestones she will have to clear to achieve her goal. Starting backward tends to help students become excited about the reward, but also unveils the important obstacles and work required to realize their ambitions.
>
> —ANTHONY HERNANDEZ, BOARD PRESIDENT, GINA'S TEAM, AND THE FIRST IN HIS FAMILY TO GRADUATE FROM COLLEGE (HARVARD)

PARACHUTE TIP

If you'd like to see how setting goals for yourself can help you bring about future success, but are unsure how to make it happen, enlist the help of an adult—someone you trust who has achieved goals similar to yours. With your goal coach, brainstorm ideas for a very short-term goal—say, thirty days. Brainstorm what you need to do every day to achieve your goal. Put those steps on a calendar you can't overlook (one that's either right in your face or on your smartphone).

and also inquire as to the institutions from which they prefer to hire graduates." In all the years I've been giving talks to parents and career practitioners, this was the first time someone had summarized this part of my message out loud (and so well).

The best career development is done backward. You identify your goals and build out your strategy backward from the future to the present.

If you haven't yet done this backward career building, start today. Whether you are in high school, college, graduate school, the military service, an apprenticeship, or the middle of your job search, make sure you *plan backward.*

Write down each step. Trace the possible outcome of each step to be sure that all you are doing now connects you to and helps create your hoped-for future.

> What you get by achieving your goals is not as important as what you become by achieving your goals.
> —HENRY DAVID THOREAU, AUTHOR OF *WALDEN*

A TOOL FOR LIFE

Goal setting isn't something you do once. You'll find that the goals that interest you change over time. Setting goals and developing to-do lists to accomplish them is a lifelong process. Knowing how to set and achieve goals is an important life tool. The goals you set and work toward shape your life.

CHAPTER 8

SOCIAL MEDIA
the new normal

Social media—the websites and applications used for social networking—differs from traditional media in that it invites interaction. Social media is all about connection, communication, and conversation. If you aren't among the small group that doesn't go online (7 percent of teens and young adults from twelve to twenty-nine years of age), you already know that. If you've used social media to check in with friends, crowd-source new TV shows to watch, play a group online game, or meet other young adults with similar interests, you already know how it feels to have a go-to network. Excellent! Having used the Web for social interaction or research projects, you under-stand how quickly it can whip information to your screen. This is why using the Internet for career information and job hunting is so effective.

Social media has superpowers that can help you explore careers, meet people whose work interests you, and uncover internships and even job openings. You can also use social media sites to create an online job-search support group, tweet your career action plans to friends, create blogs about your interests, or share your job-search frustrations.

In this chapter, we'll explore these uses of social media: how to build a bulletproof web presence, connect with useful career information, expand your network, hunt jobs, and set up LinkedIn and Twitter accounts—and stay safe doing it.

A WORLD OF POSSIBILITY

Most teens and young adults know the real details about very few types of jobs. That's true for older workers as well. The ability to gain career information expanded exponentially with the Internet, and social media has expanded access to information givers even further. Different streams of information that could have taken you months to assemble before social media can be found in a few days.

The Internet has unlimited potential for multiplying connections through web-based groups. With the Web, six degrees of separation has dropped to 4.74. That's the average number of connections you'll need to find anyone in the world. That's right—*anyone*. Very likely, degrees of separation will keep losing decimals. Now there's no excuse for not meeting living heroes, role models, or that one person you know you would love to ask, "How did you do that?"

To get the most out of using social media sites that are new to you, you will want to go slowly, getting familiar with the sites available. At first, join just one or two. As you learn more about what you want to find out or accomplish through social networking, you can be more discriminating in the sites you join and spend time on.

REALITY CHECK

You'll want to start gathering the information you need to create your online presence right now. Putting together your online profile takes more thought, time, and attention than you might expect. The Discovery Exercises in this chapter might take a week to finish—and you never know when you'll stumble across an opportunity.

GET STARTED: CREATE A SOLID
WEB PRESENCE TO BUILD YOUR BRAND

Think out the image you want to project. It's easier to start out with a good offensive strategy for your online persona than to lose opportunities and have to enact damage control. Make the image you project to the world appropriate, both for your age and for public viewing.

There are dozens of blogs, tweets, and Internet marketing impresarios to give you ideas about how to craft your brand (that's *you*, by the way). The old rule about having just one chance to make a good first impression takes on intense new meaning with social media. Building your network with social media also lets you feel how small the world has gotten. Join any site or group associated with your job interests and you may be contacted by people from anywhere in the world. Make sure you're putting your best self forward.

- **You don't have to start from scratch.** Ask friends, older siblings, coworkers, parents, and friends' parents whether they have used social media sites for career exploration, information, or job hunting. If they have, you might want to ask for their help in setting up your profile or ask to see their profiles as models. (If you enjoyed your time working with this person, consider asking him or her to be a career contact!) Check out the profiles of some of the gurus in your favorite fields or industries. What can you learn from how they present themselves?

- **What's in a name?** On social media, the name you use can lead to opportunities found or lost. You want people to look at your sites and be impressed with you, not negatively reacting to you. Use a legal name or variations of it to create your social media pages. No monikers such as Leticia *Bunny* Brown or Amos *BadBoy* Jones.

- **Ditto for e-mail handles.** Create an e-mail address appropriate for the business world. Your first and last name run together, first initial and last name run together, or name of your company if you've started a business. This is not the time to use a silly, risqué nickname.

- **Be worth a thousand words.** People looking up others on social media really, really look at pictures. These folks will make quick decisions about your character and competence based on what they see.

Headshots are considered the most professional. Choose clothing and background colors that make you look good, not washed out. No skin showing below your neck. Arms are covered. Young women can wear a blouse or dress and cardigan or jacket, and light makeup. Guys, always visually acceptable are white or blue shirts with tie and sport coat.

PARACHUTE TIP

Currently, Twitter and Instagram are the most popular social media sites among teens and young adults; Facebook not so much. Although no longer prime cool, don't overlook Facebook. From acrobats to zookeepers, from someone in your town to someone on the opposite side of the world, you can learn about jobs or a new place to live. Rather than take down your Facebook account, clean it up so it has a professional look, and use it frequently for career information, exploration, and planning.

Rotate headshots with a clear picture of you in a lab coat, tinkering in your robotics class, designing at your computer, wearing a company uniform or jacket, or putting a horse you've trained through its paces. Use the images you select to spotlight your interests.

To both genders: No gang style, no hand gestures, no sloppy pants. Take out large gem studs of any kind anywhere on your face or head. You are not auditioning for *American Idol* (unless you are). Look like someone who wants to get hired.

REALITY CHECK

What does "professional" look like anyway?

The word is an adjective, so it describes. Here are synonyms for it: expert, able, accomplished, masterful, polished, skilled, proficient, competent, practiced, trained, business-like, ethical, appropriate, fitting, correct.

Here are a couple of antonyms: amateurish and inappropriate. For example: If you list your interests as partying and snogging; if you display hand signs in your photos; if you send sexts or underdressed selfies, you are being inappropriate, amateurish, and unprofessional.

CLEAN UP YOUR ACT

Understand that the Internet is forever. Some people have posted compromising images of themselves on the Web that someday their grandchildren will see. Has that thought ever crossed their minds? Do they not care? Most adults have had a scrape or two in their youth that they'd not like to have revealed, much less circling the globe into infinity. With the Web, images sent out innocently can come back to hurt. Here's how to make sure that doesn't happen.

• **Google your name.** Take a look at what managers of local stores, college admissions officers, scholarship committees, armed service recruiters, job recruiters, human resource personnel, and others will see if they look you up online. Remember that just about anyplace considering you for a job, or reviewing an application of any sort, will look you up online. If you ask someone for career information through a social media site, you can take it as given that they will check out your online presence, too. What will they find?

Learn who else has your same name and what's on their social media sites. If someone else with your name has been arrested or has raunchy or racy pictures on her or his site, you want to know and ward off potential rejections by making it clear that you are not that person.

- **Don't let friends narrow your options.** If one of your friends is totally outrageous, has extremely blatant prejudices that she doesn't mind talking about anywhere, or likes to take unauthorized iPhone photos of you and other friends, block this person from posting on your career sites.

- **Use business manners in all of your communication.** Your texts, IMs, and posts to friends' sites may be full of abbreviations, emoticons, jokes, and maybe even colorful language. But when you contact people for career-related reasons (on the Internet or in real time), you must maintain professional language and manners at all times. If you don't know what professional manners are, type the phrase "professional manners" or "business manners" into a search engine. Read three to five articles written in the last twelve months. Go back another year if not enough articles are available in this year.

Why the emphasis on etiquette? Didn't that die out with hippies? Emphasis in the business world is not on who's cool today. Everyone's focus is on getting work done, and that means focusing on fostering productive relationships of mutual respect with colleagues and customers.

The worlds of education and work are made up of people of all backgrounds, cultures, races, and countries who may or may not share your worldview, much less your sense of humor. Since each impression you make counts, knowing and using language and behavior that is considered businesslike keeps you from making mistakes you won't be able to correct.

REALITY CHECK

Remember the Michael Phelps bong-breathing shot that rocketed around the Internet? That betrayal cost Mr. Phelps a couple million in endorsement contracts. Never trust anyone with a photo device in an embarrassing situation. Bullying of any sort is repugnant, but avoid deliberately creating a situation in which you could be the victim.

DISCOVERY EXERCISE

DESIGN YOUR WEB PRESENCE
OR REBUILD YOUR SITE

Designing your web presence is a project you can finish in three to six months. Here are a few steps:

☐ Give some thought to the image you want to project.

☐ Clean up all your website pages so they look professional.

☐ Do an online search of your name to see what potential employers will find.

☐ Pick appropriate photographs to represent you on different sites and for avatars.

☐ Set up an e-mail address on Google or Yahoo. (LinkedIn has its own message system for people you know.)

☐ Set profile privacy settings to allow communication only among those you friend or approve.

☐ If you are fourteen or older, set up a LinkedIn account.

Set a date for when you would like to have each of the above steps completed, and write it down to the left of the check box. As you finish each item in the checklist, write down its completion date. Comparing the two dates—your intention and when you really finished—will help you make better estimates of how long a project can take.

Keep a record of all your information in one (or more!) secure place:

• What e-mail addresses did you choose?

• What user names did you choose?

• What are your passwords?

PARACHUTE TIP

When setting up your own website, think in terms of screen size. What device are your intended viewers using? Smartphone, minicomputer, or—gasp—something as old-fashioned as a laptop? In the first three to six inches of screen, you need to make the connection between the job you seek and how well you can do it. Contact info can come after. Business e-mail is de rigueur. So is including a phone number at which messages can be left (and you will get them). You never need to use your physical address.

STAND OUT WITH A VISUAL RESUME

There's almost nothing more boring visually than a traditional words-on-paper resume. But with new apps, programs, and access to infinite Internet resources, you can create a riveting visual resume that can grab an employer's attention and get seen. Infographic resumes, Prezi, and Slideshare are just some of the sites already in use. Even Pinterest has taken a turn toward becoming a job-search tool. Ignore this trend at your peril: job hunters are already moving toward this new generation of online resumes.

What goes in a visual resume? Your online resume is a visual summary of what you want people to know about you, your accomplishments, or your higher education goals. It may be a series of eye-catching slides, each containing an important tidbit of information about you (what you're interested in, activities you're involved with, skills you've developed). It might be an infographic or timeline of your achievements and qualifications. Do an Internet search for "visual resumes," and dozens of images and sites will pop up. A good visual resume isn't built overnight, so spend some time experimenting and making a model before you really need one. While still keeping it professional, have a little fun with it! That may make it more enjoyable for the viewer.

You want social media to attract attention to your strengths. If what you have to say about yourself is interesting and compelling, someone just may take three minutes and learn about you. Give a visual summary that speaks to what you know and what you can do. If you have photographs or video of your participation in projects, competitions, or activities in your favorite interests, include it. Provide specific examples of where you learned necessary skills, procedures, or information, and keep it up-to-date.

A visual resume should tell the story of your qualifications and experience in a way that makes you look highly qualified to a program administrator or employer. You want your visual resume to show what you can do for employers. All of your images and graphics should be supportive of the kind of work you want to do. A picture of you in the kind of clothing appropriate for the work you want to do might even encourage a viewer to think about what opportunities he could find for you.

These days, it's almost impossible to stand out using paper resumes (see Parachute Tip). If your favorite field is crowded with people who have the same job goal as you, a visual resume on Twitter, Instagram, LinkedIn, or Pinterest may just get you noticed.

PARACHUTE TIP

A traditional paper resume should not be relied on to get you interviews. Odds are 1,471 to 1 that they will. That's an estimate of the average number of resumes circulating for each interview invitation issued. The paper resume will soon be dead. For an example as to why, check out http://blogs.vmware.com/careers/2011/10/how-a-sliderocket-employee-landed-her-dream-job.html.

SOCIAL MEDIA IS AN EXCELLENT CAREER-PLANNING TOOL

Social media works exceedingly well for gathering information about careers. For some, it's been an excellent way to find contacts and jobs. Like all tools, there are efficient and inefficient ways to use it. Below are some tips for applying what you've learned about career research and network building to the world of social media.

Reach Out for Career Information

Too many people try to get interviews before they know enough about a company or job title to do well in a hiring interview. In a hiring interview, you want to sound like someone who already has the job. That doesn't mean you act cocky; it means that by learning about all the issues surrounding a particular kind of work, you gain information that helps you talk to a potential employer in a convincing way. Social media sites like LinkedIn, Facebook, and Twitter are great ways to get this information. People who work at a place you might want to work, have jobs in a field you think would suit you, or live somewhere you'd like to know more about are all just four to seven clicks away.

Through expanding your social network contacts, it's easy to connect with people who can answer your questions about fields and jobs of interest to you. But be sure to do your homework first: read enough information about the person, company, job, or field that you don't take up a new contact's valuable time asking about basic information that could be found anywhere. Your questions should show that you've thought about this topic quite a bit.

Who's on your list? That depends on what you need to know right now to advance your career choices.

• Who do you want to meet?

• What information will help you expand your job options?

• What jobs best match your ideas about earning a good living?

• Do these jobs tend to be in a particular economic sector? Which one?

• What organizations or foundations have goals similar to yours?

• Who are the top ten people to watch in your field?

• What do you want to know from them?

• Where can you volunteer to get experience?

These are ideas to help you make a list of questions that you want to ask others who share your interests. Tell your contacts you'd like their help getting a career question answered. Post the question. You'll have help quickly.

REALITY CHECK

Using social media sites to build a network of professional contacts may be the best job-search strategy of the twenty-first century.

Job Hunting Through Network Building

Using the same network-building protocol that you would for finding career information, you can also find job-shadowing opportunities, internships, volunteer work, training and education programs, and even jobs through social media.

Making a new friend adds one person to your network. To get enough information for a successful job hunt, you need access to dozens of people. Start by making connections through existing friends. Through use of social media sites, you can grow your information network very quickly.

Your contact lists should keep evolving as you go through the different stages of job hunting. Every six months, review whom you follow and the value of their posts. Some contacts will be great at finding job openings. Others will be good at the hand-to-hand personal sales that make up a good hiring interview. Do you know what you need to know to move your career along? If not, this is another good question for your contacts to help you answer.

Here's how to finesse job hunting via social media contacts:

• Don't ask a new contact for a job outright. Executives and hiring managers at high-profile (and not-so-high-profile) companies are hit up for jobs all the time. So are the well-known employers on your town's main streets. You'll stand out if you *don't* ask.

• Use messages and posts to learn about a company or a person, or what's happening in a particular job, field, or industry: "What's happening in Industry Q in Country Z?"

• Introduce yourself and ask questions that will lead to a positive interchange.

• Get suggestions for becoming more employable in your favorite fields.

• Once you have a good relationship with your contacts, you can ask more directly about job opportunities in the fields they have worked in or know about. Would they recommend you for such a job?

• Even better—if they think you are competent and won't shame their name—one or more of your contacts may bring up job opportunities on their own.

Social Media Makes Finding Mentors Easier

Teens, young adults, and even adults without much work experience will rarely be hired beyond an entry-level job in their favorite fields. Entry-level jobs give you the opportunity to show what you can do for an employer, but you'll want to lay the groundwork for moving forward. As you'll learn throughout this book, mentors can help you build a plan to get the education or training you need for the next steps to build your career.

Successful adults often have mentors or coaches to guide their lives. Mentors can listen to your goals and help you communicate them. Mentors use

PARACHUTE TIP

If the thought of contacting someone totally terrific at what she does makes you think, "cool!" you're on board with it. If you'd rather be grounded for a month, you need to study and become good at asking questions of social media interest groups. This is an adult survival skill that you will need to use over and over again in your life. You can do this!

If you have a question or curiosity about an article or post you read, one of your groups may be able to help. Maybe you have already contacted an author and gotten no response, or gotten a response you don't quite understand—just ask for help! Here's an example of what you might post:

> *Fellow apiarists doing coding: In Mumina Zymbraun's recent article on bee-bots, she noted some of the coding issues. However, she did not mention how code was developed using flower color to influence bee-bot pollination choices. Does anyone know how that was done?*
>
> *Sincerely, Rebecca Gomez*

their experience and contacts to maximize your options, and guide you in creating a strategy for finding your dream job.

Know your next step or career goals but don't feel inclined to share those goals with the adults around you? If people for you to model your life on are as rare as armadillos in Alaska, social media is a terrific way to meet people who can and will help.

DESIGN AND BUILD A LINKEDIN PROFILE

LinkedIn is currently the premier social media site used in business. Most ambitious employees, employers, recruiters, college admissions committees, successful entrepreneurs, and those who want to be successful entrepreneurs use LinkedIn.

In some countries, you can be as young as thirteen and set up an account on LinkedIn. In most English-speaking countries, including the United States, you must be fourteen to do so.

Why? Isn't LinkedIn for old people? Not anymore. LinkedIn is encouraging high school students to set up a profile, make contacts, and use those contacts to make career and higher education decisions. Potential employers will expect to find you there. Potential contacts will be impressed that you are there.

PARACHUTE TIP

Ask your career mentors if they know of websites or groups for your field or interests. Also get suggestions for friends on Facebook, contacts through LinkedIn, or names to follow on Twitter. Your links don't have to be career oriented, but don't limit them to celebrities either. Find people whose lives fascinate you. Most will have social media accounts. Many blog. Learning about their mistakes and triumphs will jump-start your own ideas.

Go to LinkedIn and set up your profile. One great advantage of LinkedIn is that your connections can contact you and you them through LinkedIn messages. You don't have to share a personal e-mail address. This helps give younger teens (and their parents) confidence in the safety of having a LinkedIn account (although, once you start job hunting for an after-school job or an entry-level one in your favorite field, you will need to have and give an e-mail address so that employers may contact you directly).

Speaking of connections, it's time to build that list! Here are some tips.

Build Your Contact List

But I don't have any contacts! Oh yes, you do. Everyone has between 150 and 250 friends or acquaintances. Each of your friends has 150 to 250 friends and acquaintances, too. It's the people your friends know who can often connect you to the information you need. When you read phrases such as, "leverage your LinkedIn account," what's being talked about is using your contacts to get a question answered or asking your contacts to check with their contacts.

Your first list of contacts is easy to put together. Ask people you know to connect with you on LinkedIn. Consider friends of your family, relatives, teachers of the subjects you'd like to use in your work, scout leaders you work well with, managers of places you've worked, authors of blogs or magazine articles that you read regularly, heads of local, national, or even international professional associations . . . the list is endless. Most will say yes. Go searching for these people on LinkedIn and ask them to connect with you. If possible, avoid using a canned greeting. If it's someone you know but haven't seen in over a year, include references that can help that person remember who you are and how you met.

Find Groups to Follow

Whether it's an employer, an admissions officer, or a scholarship selection committee, the people who view your LinkedIn profile expect to see you connected to online communities or groups that show you are pursuing the interests that you say are important to you.

Once you have your LinkedIn account set up, click on the Interests tab. Do searches of People, Companies, and Groups. Scroll down and click on Groups. Find and join groups that deal with your career or job interests. You can just read posts for a while and get to know the group. Once someone makes a comment you like or have a question about, make contact, introduce yourself, ask to connect, and see what you can learn.

Professors are always encouraging their students to be on and use LinkedIn. If you build and use your LinkedIn profile now, you will be near to expert by the time you graduate from high school.

PARACHUTE TIP

If you send out a request on LinkedIn or other social-networking sites, always reply to every response you get. Blowing people off is a sure way to get blown off in the future. People who give you the name of a contact are risking their reputation with that person. Regardless of your interest in the information they gave you, send at least a brief, polite follow-up message for every name you are given. You are thanking this person for his time, not necessarily for his information, and you just never know when your follow-up will open a door. Those who don't follow up don't find many open doors.

Check Out University Pages

University Pages at LinkedIn were started so high school juniors and seniors could learn more about academic institutions they might want to attend. Through University Pages, you can find people's majors, where they work now, and how they feel about their time at a particular university or college. If you are thinking about getting a bachelor's degree but are unsure of what school you want to attend, once you've set up your LinkedIn profile, find the University Pages for the schools that interest you and start making contacts with alumni. The people listed on these pages have put their names up because they want to answer questions from students just like you. You may also be able to contact career center personnel and even professors to ask about educational recommendations and job prospects for potential majors.

LinkedIn has yet to start similar pages for technical schools or community colleges, so you'll have to dig a bit for information on these schools. You can start by looking at your high school's Facebook page. You may be able to find alumni from your high school who went into a branch of service, have a job, or attended a community college about which you are curious. Through Facebook, you may also be able to connect with your high school's booster club, which is made up of people who work or live in your community who want to help the school and its students. Attend a booster club or school board meeting and ask if you can have agenda time to announce that you'd like to meet people who (fill in the blank). Collect names, business cards, and e-mail addresses.

Be sure to send a thank-you e-mail to all new contacts who answer your questions, even if their information was not that helpful to you. You are thanking them for time spent on your behalf. Your gratitude will encourage them to help other high school students or young adults.

PARACHUTE TIP

LinkedIn is currently the most popular site for posting about careers. Here are some of the things you can accomplish through a LinkedIn account:

Access term papers, science fair projects, thesis papers, Eagle or other scouting projects, articles, senior projects, or other examples of your outstanding work on Google Docs. Then connect Google Docs to your LinkedIn profile. If you have made things, created pictures, or written short stories or poetry, post pictures, documents, or slide shows of these as well.

EXPERIMENT WITH TWITTER
FOR CAREER EXPLORATION

Set up a Twitter account for career exploration. Make a list of your ideas to use Twitter. Think out your look. Run your choice of headshots by a friend. What do you want to say about yourself and your career search that will be public? Which privacy settings will you use on your site? Share this information with a trusted, media-savvy adult and hear his or her suggestions, too. The more thought you give to the details of presenting yourself online before you hit *Publish*, the quicker you can finish this step and get on to using your account to learn about careers.

REALITY CHECK

All social media has a downside. For example, Twitter can be used to check up on current employees. You may have seen a TV or blog headline about someone who posted an angry rant on her personal Twitter account that was later seen by her employer. Poof! She was gone, as in fired. If you are employed or run your own business, make sure you don't get too flamboyant with your Twitter (or other social media) posts. There's weird that will get you noticed and up your visibility in a good way, and there's weird that will get you put into social media's equivalent of Siberia.

TWITTER

As if social media in general didn't bring enough excitement to the Internet, some bright spark (Jack Dorsey) thought the added challenge of limiting posts to 140 characters would make blogging even more fun. This microblogging began as a way to stay in touch, using posts called *tweets* to answer the question "what's happening?" and ended up creating a whole new subset of social media.

Because revenues from traditional media advertising were dwindling, the commercial world was quick to adopt social media advertising. Twitter became all the rage for businesses seeking new ways to advertise. Some businesses were successful using Twitter marketing, while some have made avoidable mistakes. Individuals and Twitter stars have made flaming media missteps as well. (However, you don't need to repeat them—at least not all of them! See the tips earlier in this chapter for keeping your social media presence professional.) Twitter has also become very popular as a site through which one can expand career contacts and clients, search for jobs, and check out current and potential employees and employers.

If you want to try out Twitter for career exploration or job hunting, create an account. Think out a Twitter campaign before you start it! Use your real name and a headshot of yourself in a smart blouse, sweater, shirt and tie, or jacket. You can use the logo of your business if you have one. Link your Twitter career exploration account to an equally professional e-mail address. First initial and last name, both first and last name (with or without underscores or dashes), your business name, or your interest sector, such as *Rocket engineer2b*, all can be used to create business-appropriate screen names.

STAY SAFE USING SOCIAL MEDIA

One upside of using a site you are already on to explore careers is that you are connected to people you trust. (If there are people you are connected to whom you do not trust, block them.) Through friends on your site or sites, it's likely that you'll be able to connect with people who have greater experience or even more current information than what you've read so far.

Asking questions of others who have gone down the path you are considering lets you uncover details you might not have been able to on your own.

But before you dash off a post asking about circus jobs, you need to carefully plan how to minimize any risk to yourself. For your safety, think out how much access you will allow to new contacts. What image of you will they see when they contact you? What should you reveal about yourself and your career search? Which privacy settings will you use to limit who sees this information?

Since many of your friends and classmates will also be using social media to get career information for their post–high school plans, consider asking a teacher if time can be scheduled for a class discussion about safely using social media sites and setting up positive social media profiles. If none of your teachers is social media savvy, find another adult with social media smarts. Hear out his suggestions for how to keep yourself safe while exploring this powerful new access to career information.

If, despite your best efforts, someone you're in contact with online creeps you out, cease all contact and send all correspondence to one of your parents or to an adult you trust. The world is full of wonderful and terrible people. May you meet far more of the first kind. You need a plan for presenting yourself online that minimizes the chance of your meeting the second kind.

PARACHUTE TIP

If you are under eighteen, ask a parent or other trusted adult to be in your profile picture. Consider asking this person to be your mentor as you set up and monitor your social media accounts.

EXPERT ADVICE

USING ONLINE TOOLS TO START (OR JUMP-START) YOUR CAREER PATH

Patti Wilson, MA, founder of the Career Company
Patti@pattiwilson.com
www.careercompany.com
www.linkedin.com/in/pattiwilson

The Internet is a vital hub of educational and career information, resources, opportunities, and contacts. It's also the main way that medium- and large-sized companies recruit talent, using their own web pages and widely known sites like Careerbuilder.com,

Hotjobs.com, and Monster.com. Many local businesses now use small job sites like Craigslist.com for hiring. And of course, they all use Google searches to find out more about promising job candidates.

Competition for entry-level jobs and internships is fierce. To stand out, you must create the strongest and most professional web presence possible. Here are five tips you can use right now to give your career path a boost.

Own Your Name

It's never too early to buy your name as a URL address, aka: www.firstnamelastname.com. Grab it before somebody else does! (If it's already gone, try .net, .info, .biz, .me . . .)

You can also set up e-mail addresses on Yahoo, Gmail, and Outlook now to ensure that you have them when you need them later on in your work life.

Eventually you'll want to use your URL for a professional website, a portfolio of work, or a blog. This will help college admissions staff, recruiters, and hiring managers find you in a Google search.

Aim to be found by a name search on the first page of Google by the time you graduate from college.

Build a Cone of Silence

Start managing your online privacy *now* to protect your reputation. It's crucial to selectively control who sees you, and where, online. You want only appropriate information about you to be found by a name search.

The best way to conceal your real identity is to use a disguised name on sites such as Snapchat, Instagram, Twitter, Justin.tv, and Minecraft. On any site where you must use your real name, like Facebook, set your privacy settings high to build a cone of silence around you, choosing carefully who is able to see posts and photos. Of course, your privacy settings should be set to provide no direct access to you via e-mail, phone, or offline address. The exception to this is job sites where you enter an e-mail address and a cell phone number when applying for a position.

Never put down a full street address on an online resume—just city and state or a landline phone number.

Create a Digital Footprint

The first impression colleges and companies have of you can be enhanced by your online comments on blog postings, news articles, or even book reviews. By sharing your opinions online, you build a brand for yourself that can keep on growing with you. Be selective in the online sites and magazine articles you choose—you are creating your persona and reputation with every comment.

You can include links to articles and books that you have commented on in your resume.

Start a Search for Jobs

Reading job postings of companies who make products and deliver services that you like and use can lead to ideas for classes to take and majors to pursue. You have to dig into the career pages of many companies, not just a few, to uncover and learn about the range of jobs out there.

Don't wait until you graduate. Start with the websites you frequent, and expand from there.

Join LinkedIn.com

LinkedIn's website design is quiet and low-key, not flashy. But with nearly three hundred million members, it's the eight-hundred-pound gorilla in the room for finding and being found for jobs. One of the best things you can do for the future of your employment is to join LinkedIn and put up a profile while you're still in high school.

There are sites similar to LinkedIn.com in Europe (www.Viadeo.com and www.Xing.com), Asia (www.Apnacircle.com and www.Tianji.com), and Latin America (www.Orkut.com). Join and establish your profile there if you are seeking an internship or full-time work outside the United States.

Set a goal to have five hundred connections on LinkedIn by the time you graduate from college—they will be the support team for your job search.

Are you ready to learn how to land your dream job? Great! All the work you've done in the earlier chapters of this book provides a foundation for this next important step. In part 1, you became a detective in your own life, finding clues that revealed your dream job (or field) by identifying your interests, best skills, favorite types of people, and ideal work environments. In part 2, you explored ways to continue the journey toward your dream job by making the most of high school and higher education, and using tools like goal setting and social networking.

Now we'll dive into the depths of job hunting. First, we explore concrete ways to make your job hunt more efficient, effective, and successful (chapter 9). Then we look at the scoop on hiring interviews (chapter 10). Since many of you will find success in careers not yet imagined, next we'll explore career trends (chapter 11). Finally, we put the search for your dream job in the larger context of your whole life (chapter 12). We invite you to consider who you want to be, what you most want to do in life, and how you can use your talents to make the world a better place to live.

> Always be a first-rate version of yourself, instead of a second-rate version of somebody else.
> —JUDY GARLAND, SINGER AND ACTRESS

part three

LAND YOUR DREAM JOB
create your ideal life . . . and more

I wish that someone had told me that success comes more easily if you are doing a job that you truly enjoy and not to pursue a career that seems "safe" if it is going to make you miserable. People have said that forever. Apparently this needed to be pounded into my head.

—JULIE PORTEOUS LEACH, AUDITOR, AGE 29

CHAPTER 9

SEARCH FOR YOUR DREAM JOB
finding the best fit

Job hunting is both exciting and scary. The process becomes an adventure when you look at all the elements of your parachute and say, "I wonder how these all come together in a job?"

With your parachute finished, it's hard not to be curious about names of jobs that will fit you well. What are those jobs called? Do similar positions exist in different fields? Knowing answers to these questions puts you ahead of most job-seeking young adults. A set of overlapping circles is called a *Venn diagram*. The Venn diagram to the right shows you what you must find to achieve your goal of a job you will enjoy.

WHAT, EXACTLY, *IS* A DREAM JOB?

Everyone has an opinion as to the definition of the term *dream job.* We're sure you have yours. In this book:

1. *Dream job* is not used to describe a fantasy job that you don't have the temperament for. Fantasize about being a trauma surgeon, but you're a Doc Martin type? Being an ER surgeon is not a dream job for you.

2. *Dream job* does not mean an impossible expectation for your level of skill. Excel in basketball? Okay, at what level of competition? Unless you are Olympic material, the NBA won't preemptively draft you in the ninth grade. That's simply never happened.

3. A dream job is one that you *can get.* If you work hard at your plan for career development, landing your dream job—or getting really close—is going to happen.

DIFFERENCES BETWEEN A *GOOD JOB* AND A *DREAM JOB*

A *good job* you enjoy most days. A good job pays well given your level of skill and the going rate in the marketplace. A good job uses many of your best skills.

A *dream job* is one that you love. It feels like learning, work, and play all rolled together. A dream job tempts you to say you'd do the job for no pay. In a dream job, the pay is good (again, given your level of skill and market demand). Your dream job uses 75 percent of your favorite skills, incorporates your interests, and aligns with your values. (The identification of these factors as vital to career satisfaction comes from longtime Alaskan and Parachute practitioner Deeta Lonergan.)

At times in your life, you may need to take a good job or a barely okay one. But always try to find the best job you can in the labor market you're in—after all, it takes the same amount of effort to find a job you won't like as a job you will. And if you don't like your job, you won't work hard enough to be a success: in the business world, it's those who do the equivalent of A- and B-level work who get promoted.

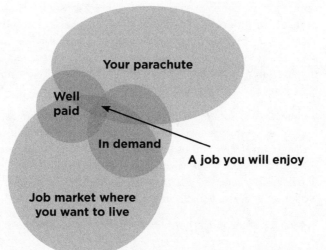

PARACHUTE TIP

Here are four steps to your dream job:

Step 1: Conduct information interviews.

Step 2: Cultivate contacts and create networks.

Step 3: Research organizations of interest.

Step 4: Begin a campaign to get the job you want.

Repeat these steps with each job target in each field that fascinates you. A good job search has three related job targets.

FOUR STEPS TO YOUR DREAM JOB

Let's go through the steps—some of which you'll recognize from earlier chapters—that will help you land the job of your dreams.

Step 1: Conduct Information Interviews

Too many people make their job hunt harder by starting in the wrong place: they try to get hiring interviews before they know their best skills, much about the job market, what jobs they want, or how to present themselves. But you've already done the exercises in part 1 and identified either three potential dream jobs or three areas of interest; you've made sure these jobs or fields still interest you; and you've reviewed and updated your parachute. You're ready to look for your first full-time job! The first step is to do lots of information interviews. You learned the basics of interviewing for information in chapter 4 and the fundamentals of social networking in chapter 8. Now you'll build on those basics.

Remember, information interviewing shouldn't be complicated or intimidating. As we've said before, it's just a conversation with another person about a shared interest or enthusiasm—in this case, a particular job or career. You ask questions, but you'll spend most of your time listening. Let the people you're interviewing tell you their stories about how they came to do the work that interests you. Soon you'll know

• More about the industry or field in which this job happens.

• Common salaries for this work.

• Whether this is a good career choice for you.

• Employers who hire people to do this work.

• Ideas for how you can train for or get such a job.

Information interviews will reveal whether or not your best skills match the most common activities or tasks done in a particular job and how much the work overlaps your interests. Before you ask people to talk with you, read several descriptions of that job, field, industry, or career. You will ask better questions and be a better listener. The information you collect will make more sense. For each person with whom you have an information interview, use Google or LinkedIn to see what you can learn about them. What you read about an interviewee's background, experience, education, or current position will help focus your questions. Also, your interviewees will be impressed (maybe even flattered) that you took the time to research them.

BASIC INFORMATION INTERVIEW QUESTIONS

- What do you do? What are three to five of the most common tasks or activities you do each day? What skills do you use doing those tasks? Do you mind the repetition?
- How long have you been doing this work?
- How did you get into this work?
- What kind of training or education did you need for this job? How much did it cost?
- What do you like about your job? What don't you like about your job?
- What are the main challenges in this industry?
- What do you see happening in this field in the next five to ten years?
- What is your ultimate career goal?
- What is the starting salary in this job or field? What is the salary range with three to six years' experience?
- Do you have any additional comments, suggestions, or advice?
- Can you give me the names of two or three other people who do this same work?

So in this first step, find and talk to people who have jobs or careers that interest you. (These interviews are *in addition* to ones you may have done earlier, in high school, when you were just beginning to research jobs and careers.) If you've targeted three to five potential dream jobs, continue your research by talking with people who do the job you want to do or who work in the same field for each of your dream jobs. Talking with people gives you a reality check for what you've read about a job or your occupational preferences. These conversations will help you determine how well each target matches your parachute. The job that matches best becomes your #1 job target, the job that matches next best becomes your #2 job target, and so on. Try to find at least three kinds of jobs or careers that overlap with your parachute.

Want to see some interviews in action? Following are transcripts of information interviews with two young adults.

── INFORMATION INTERVIEWS ──

JOB FAMILY: PRODUCTION/MANUFACTURING

Name: Matthew F. Sargent. **Age:** 27. **Job title:** Distiller. **Holland code:** RIA. **Field:** Beverage Alcohol Manufacture. **Degrees (not used in current job):** BA Political Science, BS Meteorology. **Employer(s):** Headframe Spirits. **Education or training for this job?** Chemistry, Food Sciences, and Engineering are helpful. **Salary ranges:** Starting: ~$30,000/year; three to six years' experience: ~$55,000+/year.

What do you do?

I make and distill spirits such as whiskey and vodka.

How did you get into this work?

I had a strong interest in the food sector and ended up working for and with some top-level chefs. My interest led to what accompanies food, and I moved into the beer, wine, and spirits industry.

What are the tasks you do most often?

Mash grain and other starches in an effort to produce alcohol via yeast fermentation. I then distill the mash to separate the alcohol from the yeast, grain, and water. I also proof and check the spirits in order to ensure they comply with state and federal guidelines.

Do you supervise anyone?

I currently supervise three people. All three work the bottling line, where they filter, bottle, and package our finished products.

How long have you been at this job?

Just over one year.

What do you like about your work?

I love making a product that people can drink and be delighted about. Introducing someone to a good bourbon or gin for the first time can be a real treat. Especially when they have had bad experiences with those products in the past.

What don't you like about your job?

The federal and state regulations are currently in a jumble. It makes following the law and doing paperwork a huge hassle.

What are the main challenges in this industry?

As this industry (microdistilling and microbrewing) becomes more popular, the government at both the state and federal levels is proving to be very cautious and quite conservative with the laws that it passes.

What do you see happening in this field in the next five to ten years?

The next five to ten years will be interesting. As the microdistilling boom continues, it will eventually lead to a bubble that will burst. Only those distilleries that establish themselves well and prove to have the best product will remain. This is very similar to what the microbrewing industry is currently doing.

Did you use networking or social networking to get this job?

I obtained this job exclusively through networking. I didn't even fill out a proper application for this job until nearly six months *after* I had started working.

What is your ultimate career goal?

At this juncture I do not know. I am just getting my feet wet in this industry, so it is hard to say what my ultimate career goal will be. All I know is that I love what I do.

Outside your job, what are your other interests or hobbies?

I love to work on the computer with websites and design. I also love the marketing area. Some of my hobbies include cooking, skiing, fly fishing, and fencing.

Did you have an internship in this field? If yes, was it helpful to your employment?

I did not.

What advice would you give a young adult who wants to work in your field?

Study chemistry and food science. Having a knowledgeable background in food and spirits before entering the industry is super helpful. This isn't necessarily skill, but rather research you can do on the Internet. Also have a love for beverage alcohol—and drink it responsibly!

Contact information you would like to share:

matt@headframespirits.com

JOB FAMILY: SOCIAL SERVICES

Name: Emily Wright. **Age:** 27. **Job title:** Residential Operations Assistant. **Field:** Special Education. **Employer(s):** Melmark New England. **Education or training for this job?** Bachelor's degree in social work and extensive training with the company. **Salary ranges:** Starting: $12.50/hour; three to six years' experience: $16.24 per hour; $40,600/year.

What do you do?

I work in a school and residential setting for autistic children, ages four to twenty-one. Melmark New England is based on the ideas and practices of applied behavioral analysis (ABA). My main responsibility is to manage staffing for the six residences. About 40 percent of the children who attend the day-school program are also under our twenty-four-hour care in Melmark's homes. I work with the residential staff, not the school staff.

How did you get into this work?

I have been involved in programs in the past that increased my interest in working with a special-needs population. I have done volunteer work, internships, and summer camps. As a paid employee, I worked with low-functioning adults in a day program, autistic and behaviorally challenged children in a school program, and now, autistic children in a residential program.

What are the tasks you do most often?

In my current position, I am more "behind the scenes" than working directly with the children. I create and monitor schedules to ensure that each house is fully staffed while children are present. Depending on a child's I.E.P., he or she can either require 1:1 care or be paired with another student for a 2:1 ratio, students to staff. If a staff member is ill or will be late to the shift, I will make necessary changes among the six houses so that all houses remain fully staffed. At Melmark, this is known as "meeting ratio."

Do you supervise anyone?

I supervise all residential staff attendance. I am the person of contact from 7:00 a.m. Monday to Friday at 6:00 p.m. This means anyone who is late or is ill must check with me first before he can be approved for missing a shift. If I notice a pattern in any particular staff for being consistently late, I will bring the matter to my supervisor and appropriate actions will be taken. Along with other supervisors at Melmark, I am taking a course to improve my supervision skills. We have chosen an area of weakness that we see on a daily basis.

How long have you been at this job?

I have been at this job for four months. I feel very lucky that I have the opportunity to work with Melmark. It is the first job I've had since college where I see a future. It is never a good sign to start job searching within the first year of employment. I have done that in the past. At Melmark, I see so much potential professional growth for myself. I am excited to see where I will be within the company this time next year, and the year after that.

What do you like about your work?

I like many things about my job. I love the independence I am given. I have been trained on different tasks, and once I show mastery of that task, I am left to myself to do it on my own. My supervisor will give me a new task to master when she feels I am ready to do more. She is always available to offer advice and help. I am proud of Melmark's mission to provide excellent services to their target population. It's been successful for them. I think it is so important to agree with the mission of your company.

What don't you like about your job?

This is my first job where I am not working directly with the population we serve. Although this is a nice change for me, I do miss that aspect of former jobs. I have been assured I will begin training with individual children. I will be able to work directly with them if needed.

What are the main challenges in this industry?

Melmark New England was founded in 1988. When it began, it only served children twenty-one and younger. Services for adults (persons twenty-two and older) are significantly decreased after their twenty-second birthdays. Melmark has since started a residential program for adults. This specific program offers individuals the same at-home care that we give to our twenty-one-and-younger population. The adult-services program is still growing, but with difficulty due to the restrictions by the Department of Developmental Services. Services are cut off at age twenty-two, and dependable funding for adult programs is difficult to find.

What do you see happening in this field in the next five to ten years?

Increased demand. Melmark will continue to grow. The school facility will enlarge as more children are involved. Melmark will increase its number of residential offerings. The need for services for children with special needs will grow. There will be more options for this population. I am unsure of where adult services will be in five to ten years. May it please be on par with the caliber of services for children.

Did you use networking or social networking to get this job?

No. Perhaps in the future, I will.

What is your ultimate career goal?

I would like to come back around to direct care. Melmark offers very good benefits, including education reimbursement. I plan to take classes in counseling. I would like to be working even more independently and directly with people in need.

Outside your job, what are your other interests or hobbies?

I am a very active person. My husband, Jared, and I are always doing something! We enjoy being outdoors. In July, Jared and I returned to Massachusetts after living in Mexico City for a year teaching English. It was an amazing experience that was daunting to take, but was an amazing adventure. I am a very social person, and I have a job that still allows me to be so.

Did you have an internship in this field? If yes, was it helpful to your employment?

I did three internships while earning my degree. Two internships were working with elderly populations, and the other was working in an alternative school with teens with behavioral challenges. These internships were enjoyable, but not helpful for employment. In interviews I highlighted volunteer experiences more than internships.

What advice would you give a young adult who wants to work in your field?

As clichéd as it sounds, people should do what makes them happy. I made a decision. It is more important for me to do something that I believe in and that makes me feel good than to do something for the money. Your work shouldn't be just a job—it should be your career. I am happy to wake up every day and go to work. I think I am lucky.

Contact information you would like to share:

EOlson720@gmail.com

PARACHUTE TIP

Never underestimate the value of thanking someone for meeting with you. Your name might be forgotten, but your gesture will lodge in memory under "that nice kid who sent me a thank-you note." To review the basics of writing thank-you notes, see page 55.

Step 2: Cultivate Contacts and Create Networks

The people you meet through information interviews become contacts and part of your career network. You already have a personal network of friends, family, and other people you have met; a professional or work network is necessary, too. Both networks help your job search. Keep in touch with your contacts. Send annual updates about your life or career. Show interest in their lives as well. Has someone you haven't seen in a long time ever asked you for a favor, then dropped you again? Did you feel used? The same is true of the people in your professional network. Just as preventative maintenance keeps your car running well, treating your contacts well keeps your networks healthy.

Contacts you have good relationships with become your eyes and ears. They may hear about job openings before they become public and alert you to those opportunities, and they may even put in a good word for you.

Keep contact information of people you meet—names, phone numbers, and addresses (both e-mail and physical mailing address). You may need to access them in the future. File this information in your career portfolio (see page 74).

You can ask for names of people to contact from

• Family—immediate and extended.

• Friends and parents of friends.

• Friends on Facebook or similar social media sites.

• Neighbors.

• School guidance counselors or club sponsors.

• Teachers or professors.

• Coworkers and bosses (past and present).

• People you've met through temporary or volunteer work.

• Supervisors of volunteer or school projects.

• Mentors or people you've job shadowed.

• People you've met through information interviews.

• Your pastor, rabbi, mullah, youth-group leader, or other members of your spiritual community.

• Members of community-service organizations (such as the Lions, Kiwanis, Rotary, Soroptimists, Association of University Women, and Boys and Girls Clubs).

• People you meet in line at the movies, grocery store, or on vacation.

Create a list of five contacts to start. Get three more names from each contact—then each of those contacts—and you'll soon know what's what for the work you want in the town you want to live.

> If you make ten inquiries and everyone says no one's hiring, expand your geographic boundaries, or change your target field.
> –MARTY NEMKO, CAREER COACH AND AUTHOR OF *COOL CAREERS FOR DUMMIES*

> I wish I would have asked more questions about the future of architecture before I decided to become an architect. If I had asked older architects what changes they saw coming to the field, I think I could have anticipated some of the frustrations I'm now having with my profession.
> —SCOTT J. SMABY, AWARD-WINNING ARCHITECT

Step 3: Research Organizations of Interest

Have you done enough information interviews to prioritize your job targets (step 1)? How about cultivating contacts by adding to or creating networks (step 2)? Now it's time to find out what organizations hire people to do the job you want to do in the places you want to live. If the same job is available in different work environments, which suits you best? Each information interview needs to give you enough detail about the work environment (boss, coworkers, culture, workspace) to make choices between employers. You can use these details to put together a prioritized list of the ten employers for whom you would most like to work.

Building on your information interviews, you will now research these organizations more thoroughly. In addition to a general Internet search, you can

• Visit company websites and websites for that field or industry.

• Look through the archives of newspapers or periodicals and find written information on the organizations.

• Talk to people who work for (or used to work for) organizations you're interested in. Also, talk with competitors (if this is a business) or people at similar agencies (if this is, for example, a nonprofit agency).

• Talk to the suppliers or customers of a business or a particular department of a corporation.

• Ask for information from business leaders in your community, the local chamber of commerce or private industry council, or the state employment office.

When you contact people who work for an organization, or used to work for it, you'll want to get answers to the following questions (some of which are difficult to ask directly, so be very tactful).

- What kind of work do they do there?

- What kind of goals are they trying to achieve? Are they achieving their goals? (Many organizations have mission statements. Read them!)

- What are their needs, problems, and challenges?

- What kind of reputation does the company have within their industry?

- How do they treat their employees?

As you learn more about these organizations, some places will seem more appealing to you—that's exactly what you want to find out. After you've completed your research, you'll know which organizations hire people to do the work you most want to do and which have a work environment that fits you best.

Step 4: Begin a Campaign to Get the Job You Want

From your research in step 3, choose the top five places you want to work. At each place, identify the person who has the power to hire you. In a small business, the hiring manager might be the owner. In larger businesses, department managers do hiring interviews. Phone the person who has the power to hire you and ask for a twenty-minute appointment. Be direct. Tell this person you'd like to discuss how well your strengths match the job she hires for. (No, there doesn't have to be an opening.) About 65 percent of those you call will make an appointment with you.

Before your appointment, review your parachute. Pick three to five items from your career portfolio. Rehearse how these items connect to the job your want. Make an outline of everything you know about this job, the organization, and the person interviewing you. Be ready to talk about how your skills, training, education, experience, and enthusiasm for this work will make you an outstanding employee. Keep your focus on what you can do for them. Few employers are interested in what they can do for you.

If there's a company you want to work for and you haven't learned the name of the person who has the power to hire, use all your networks to get the information you need.

If no offers of employment come from the first five organizations you targeted, select five more that have the jobs and work environments you want. Keep researching organizations, expanding the number of people in your network, talking with them, and asking for hiring interviews until you receive a job offer—or three.

JOB-SEARCH BASICS

Now that you know the four steps to finding the job you want, let's take a
closer look at some of the basics that will support and guide you.

What You Need for a Job Search

Because you aren't in control of other people's actions or decisions, the
job hunt can feel frustrating. But you can take pride in creating, organizing,
and storing your career-planning and job-search materials efficiently and
effectively. Here are some things you'll need to do that:

• A desk or table. If not available where you live, a library or coffeehouse
  will do.

• Some way of storing, organizing, printing, and retrieving information
  you gather . . . online, in a milk crate, or in a notebook. Secure your work
  safely.

• A secure and reliable way of getting phone messages from employers
  and other contacts. Make sure in your outgoing greeting you clearly state
  your first and last name. Your recorded greeting should be businesslike; no
  "Waz up at da tone." Your voice mail may be an employer's first impression
  of you—make it a good one. You may also want to mention your job search
  in your outgoing message. Here's a sample message:

  *Hi, this is Jessica Wong. I'm sorry I can't take your call right now. Please
  leave me a message after the beep. I'm currently looking for work in
  accounting at a hospital or large medical office. If you know of any
  leads or contacts for me, be sure to mention that too, along with your
  phone number. Thanks a lot.*

- An email address that you can check at least daily. Make sure it's business-like. Many public libraries provide access to the Internet and e-mail for people who don't have a computer.

- A professional online web presence, such as a LinkedIn profile, where you can post your resume, list your accomplishments, gather recommendations, and so on (see chapter 8 for tips).

- Reliable transportation, for both interviews and getting to work once you are hired.

- Appropriate interview clothes. Look at how people are dressed at places where you want to work. Wear clothing just a bit more formal than what these workers wear when you go for an information or hiring interview. If you don't have some sharp outfits for interviews, some communities have organizations that help you find good interview clothes for free or low cost.

REALITY CHECK

Do you know what you want to do for an employer? Don't start a job hunt until you can confidently discuss with employers what you can do for them. The number one question in the employers' minds is if they hire you, what do they get for their dollar? If you can't answer that question in detail with half a dozen stories to support your skills, interests, and enthusiasm, you're not ready to look for job vacancies.

First, revisit and update your parachute. When you know what you would enjoy doing to earn money in the current job market and can talk about how your skills are a great match, you are instructed to pass Go and begin your job search.

The Best Ways to Look for a Job

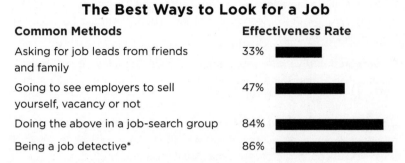

Common Methods	Effectiveness Rate	
Asking for job leads from friends and family	33%	
Going to see employers to sell yourself, vacancy or not	47%	
Doing the above in a job-search group	84%	
Being a job detective*	86%	

*A "job detective" follows the strategies used in this book: doing research on oneself, finding jobs that match skills and interests, identifying which places of employment have those jobs, and then determining who has the power to hire new staff. We are indebted to Parachute trainer Brian McIvor for this concept, explained in his book *Career Detection: Finding and Managing Your Career* (Management Briefs, 2009). The success rate of the job detective method is twelve times higher than just sending out resumes.

Tips for Savvy Job Searchers

Once you have what you need for your job search, the following techniques and suggestions will jump-start your progress.

• **Search full-time.** The more time you spend actively looking for a job, the quicker your job hunt will go.

• **Protect your job-search time.** If family and friends see that you're serious about devoting several hours a day to your job search, they should begin to honor the time you commit to finding the job that's right for you.

• **Remember that many vacancies aren't advertised.** From 75 to 80 percent of open positions aren't listed or published. Doing information interviews and letting people know what type of position you're looking for will increase your odds of success.

• **Make lots of phone calls and send lots of e-mails.** Keep at it until you've lined up at least two employers who will meet with you each day of the week.

• **Practice your pitch.** Create a twenty- to thirty-second pitch stating your name, the work you seek, and two or three of your best skills.

- **Target small organizations.** Small businesses hire 75% of US workers. If possible, begin your job search with organizations that have no more than twenty-five employees.

- **Be prepared to give references.** Employers want to know about your reliability and personality. Think about who among your network might be willing to provide a positive reference.

- **Volunteer at least one day a week.** You can get great experience—and references!—while job hunting if you volunteer at a school leadership program or club, nonprofit organization, local business, or church.

PARACHUTE TIP

When's the best time to call?

Job hunters have reported that they have success reaching employers or hiring managers in person at the following times:

- First thing in the morning and last thing in the afternoon
- Fridays right before and after lunch

What About Resumes?

Except for the section on visual resumes on page 115, this book doesn't include information on resumes because

- There are lots of other resume-writing resources (career centers, resume books, and websites).

- Resumes are not a very effective job-search tool for adults. They're even less effective for younger workers. Usually younger workers lack experience in the jobs or fields in which they most want to work.

- Resumes focus on past work history, which is mostly useful if your work history supports your next job goal; for instance, changing jobs but staying in the same field.

- People depend too much on a resume to get them a job. Never defer starting your job hunt until you have the perfect resume—it doesn't exist, and you might not need it. Spend time revising and reviewing your best skills and strengths for the job rather than laboring over a resume.

• You don't need a resume to start information interviews. If you've never done a serious job hunt or it's been a while, you need to get to know the job market again. After a dozen information interviews, you'll write a better resume.

Take Care of Yourself

A job search can be very demanding. It can wear down even the most positive person. To deal with this,

• Don't focus on your job hunt being over. Instead, keep track of which tried-and-true techniques you use. Create a chart to record how many phone calls, information interviews, hiring interviews, or new contacts you make each day. Higher numbers mean that you're conducting an effective job search. Expect a job search to last nine to twelve months—and if it takes less time, rejoice!

• Create an "advisory board" for your job search. Individually or as a group, arrange to meet once a month with people who know a lot about the industry or field you want to work in, people who are supportive and can give informed suggestions, or people who are very good at getting jobs they like (perhaps someone you met while doing information interviews).

• Take care of your physical body, too. Eat right, get enough sleep, cut down on caffeine (and drink more water), and avoid negative people. Bad health habits negatively affect how you look and your energy level. Exercise, listen to motivational tapes, see good friends, and watch movies that make you laugh or give you hope. If there are other things you enjoy doing that help you take care of yourself, incorporate them into your routine.

A job hunt can be very rewarding, but rarely is it easy. It demands physical, mental, and emotional energy. Doing a job search well takes dedicated time. Be gentle with yourself in the process. No one has to do anything right the first time.

> What accounts for the difference between greatness and mediocrity? Extraordinary drive.
> —BENJAMIN BLOOM, AUTHOR OF *DEVELOPING TALENT IN YOUNG PEOPLE*

TEN INCREDIBLY COMMON JOB-HUNTING MISTAKES MADE BY NEWBIES

- Thinking you must do this all by yourself
- Spending too little time on your job search (if you're unemployed, aim for six hours a day)
- Continuing to use techniques that aren't working
- Being financially unprepared for how long the job search really takes (budget for at least nine months)
- Ignoring successful techniques because "that's just not me"
- Having only one job target
- Limiting your job search to what's "out there"
- Giving up too easily and too soon
- Thinking someone else will do this for you
- Starting in the wrong place. Don't seek employment interviews before you are ready to be blindingly brilliant in them. Treat the job hunt as a job, not a game.

Have you made any of the mistakes above? Along with putting to use the job-search strategies and techniques you've learned in other chapters of this book, avoiding fruitless efforts will hasten a successful end to your job hunt. Knowing what *not* to do—and even more important, knowing what *to* do—will put you way ahead of less determined job hunters.

PARACHUTE TIP

Do you know of someone who is looking for work? You'll be more persistent, uncover more leads, and even have more fun if you job hunt with support from a buddy.

PARACHUTE TIP

The most effective—and least used—job-search strategy
is to know twelve people who do exactly the work you
want to do or who are employed in the industry you
hope to be. They will hear of openings before you do.
Twelve people are twelve sets of eyes and ears helping
you with your job search. Imagine all the openings you
could learn about if your network reached forty!

> Nobody in life gets exactly what they thought they
> were going to get. But if you work really
> hard and you're kind, amazing things will happen.
> I'm telling you, amazing things will happen.
> —CONAN O'BRIEN, TALK SHOW HOST

HIRING INTERVIEWS
the scoop

The best reason to know effective job-search techniques is that you'll use them frequently during your money-earning years. Researchers speculate that people your age will be in the workforce sixty years and have a score of jobs. Time will tell!

You're ready for hiring interviews if

• You've talked to a dozen people in the field or job you want.

• You've verified through reading and conversations that this work fits you.

• You've compiled a list of fifteen favorite employers.

• You know the names of and have researched the hiring managers at the top five places you want to work.

• You know appropriate stories demonstrating how you learned and use your skills.

GOAL: GET GOOD ENOUGH AT INTERVIEWS TO ENJOY THEM!

Hiring interviews can be stressful. They're often compared to blind dates. People often go to interviews without knowing anything about their "date"—the interviewers and the company, organization, or agency where they are interviewing. Don't make that mistake. Learn as much as you can about the job you want in each organization you want to hire you. The more prepared you are, the better your interviews will go.

Don't expect your interviewer to make a connection between what's on your resume and your ability to do this job. You have to tell the story of your interest in and experience for this job in a way that shows how qualified you are to do it. Young people are often surprised how hard they have to sell themselves in an interview, even when the interviewer knows them and their previous work.

Imagine that you are an employer interviewing two applicants for one job. The first seems either scared or bored. Her answers are brief. When asked why she wants the job, she replies that the pay is good and it's an easy commute. The other applicant begins by thanking you for the interview, then tells you about the classes she has taken to prepare for this work and the internships she's done to hone her on-the-job skills. When asked why she wants the job, this applicant tells you that she wants to work for your company because of its great reputation and hopes you'll hire her. But if you don't, she is going to keep applying for jobs like this because it's what she loves to do and believes she is meant to do. Which applicant would you hire?

It takes young people an average of nine information interviews before they feel comfortable enough to do it well. Imagine how many hiring interviews you will have before you feel comfortable being interviewed. If your career center doesn't do mock interviews, ask adults or friends you trust to put you through interview scenarios and questions and check out your handshake. It shouldn't be too strong or too weak. This kind of practice keeps you breathing and thinking clearly even when you're stressed.

Hiring interviews are a lot easier if you've done information interviews. You may have butterflies bombarding your innards during hiring interviews, but you've talked with people about work before. A hiring interview is simply a conversation focused on work. Your interviewer wants to know what you can do for the company; you want to tell your interviewer all that you can

PARACHUTE TIP

Take a trip to the company, business, or agency the week before your interview at the same time of day. Where is the building entrance? Which bus line gets you there, or where you can park? If you do this kind of reconnaissance before the interview, you'll be less stressed the day of the interview. The less stressed-out you are, the more confident you appear. Employers hire confident people.

do for her company. A hiring manager wants evidence that you can use your education, training, and talents to help his company achieve its goals. The more homework you've done about yourself, the job, and the needs of the organization where that job is, the more pleasant hiring interviews will be.

BEFORE YOUR INTERVIEW

Before your interview, think about these two questions:

1. What do I still need to know about this job at this organization?

2. What information do I need to communicate about myself?

There are many books and blogs that can help you prepare for typical interview questions. Practice answering these questions. Do you sound convincing? The questions your interviewer most wants answered are

• Why are you here?

• What can you do for us?

• Can I afford you?

• What kind of a person are you? Do I want you working for me and representing our program, department, or company?

• What distinguishes you from nineteen other people who can do the same tasks that you can?

PARACHUTE TIP

• Mix speaking and listening equally so the interview feels like a friendly conversation.

• Answer the interviewer's questions; don't go off on tangents.

• Speak well, if at all, of former bosses and colleagues.

No matter what questions your interviewer asks you, these five things are what he *really* wants to know. The motivation for asking is fear of making a poor hiring choice. If you know an employer's fear, you can pick examples of your skills and suitability to address these fears.

PARACHUTE TIP

Avoid these common interview mistakes:

- Arriving late
- Bad personal hygiene
- Excess cologne
- Inappropriate clothing
- Lack of initial eye contact
- Mispronouncing your interviewer's name
- Rudeness of any sort
- A weak handshake
- Keeping your iPod or MP3 player hung around your neck
- Not turning off your cell phone

DURING YOUR INTERVIEW

Personnel professionals tell us that many interviewers make up their mind about you in the first half-minute of the interview. They spend the remaining time looking for reasons to justify their decision. It's not the technical questions that get applicants eliminated. Employers consistently report that these three factors most often influence your interviewer's first impression of you:

1. Were you on time for the interview?

2. Did you look the interviewer in the eye as you greeted him or her?

3. What was the quality of your handshake?

What Interviewers Notice

A detailed study done by Albert Merhabian, PhD, at UCLA a couple of years ago revealed some surprising things about what interviewers pay attention to. It turns out that interviewers are preoccupied with nonverbal communication, to make sure it matches up with what the interviewee is saying (and if it doesn't, they're less likely to hire that applicant!).

Percentage of attention: Focused on:

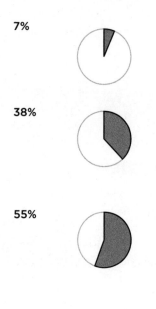

7%

WORDS
Choose your words carefully. In three different ways, explain the skills, experi-ence, or training that most qualify you for this job.

38%

VOICE QUALITY
Don't have too much caffeine before an interview. If your voice tends to get high-pitched when you're nervous, take a thermos of warm water with you and have some sips before your interview starts.

55%

NONVERBAL
(handshake, posture, what you do with your hands, nervous mannerisms, eye contact, and so on)
Don't always look your interviewer straight in the eye. This can be seen as threatening. Alternate direct looks with looking past his or her ear, slightly above the head.

During the interview, an interviewer is assessing your attitude. The way you conduct yourself in the interview gives a lot of clues as to what type of employee you'll be. An interviewer will quickly judge whether you are

• A pleasant person to be around—or not.

• Interested in other people—or totally absorbed with yourself.

• At peace with yourself and the world—or seething with anger beneath a calm exterior.

• Outgoing or introverted.

• Communicative or monosyllabic.

• Focused on giving—or only on taking.

• Anxious to do the best job possible—or just going through the motions.

Your interviewer notices whether you project energy or expend only minimal effort to engage. Do you exude curiosity or a sense of sullenness? To employers, your attitude is more important than your skills, because it signals how hard you're willing to work and whether you can work well with other people. Employers will hire someone with lesser skills but with a good attitude before they'll hire a more experienced and more skilled person with a bad attitude.

Your interviewers are judging how quickly you'll be productive if hired and how well you'll fit with the team. Tell them multiple stories that show you can use the skills they identify as essential. Expect to tell them in different ways until you sense they hear you. Just 7 percent of their attention is on your words!

> If you just focus on getting your job done and being a good colleague and a team player in an organization, and are not focused on being overly ambitious and wanting pay raises and promotions and the like . . . the rest of it all takes care of itself.
> —RICHARD ANDERSON, CEO OF DELTA AIR LINES

Interview the Interviewer

Even in a hiring interview, you are still assessing the job. You need to know, Does this job fit me? Does it use many of my strengths? Am I comfortable with the people I've met?

Ask yourself the following questions:

1. *Do I want to work with these people?* Pay attention to your intuition. Sometimes your interviewer will give all the "right" answers to your questions, but you'll still have an uneasy feeling. Don't ignore that feeling. You want an environment where you'll thrive. Carol and venture capitalist Guy Kawasaki put it starkly: "When you work for someone else, your real job is to make your boss look good." Before committing to a job, ask yourself "Is this person someone I want to make look good?" If the answer is no, keep looking.

2. *Can I do this job? Do I want to do this job?* In chapter 1, we introduced "can-do" skills and "want-to" skills. What skills are most needed in this job? Are they skills you love to use repeatedly, or just once in a while?

3. *Can I persuade the organization that I'm different from other applicants?*
   Formulate an answer to this question before you walk into the interview.
   Weave in what you know of the company's needs as you talk about your
   work style and experience.

Keep in mind that interviewers are as scared as you are during the hiring
interview. They don't want to make a hiring mistake. Companies have tales
of gruesome hiring misadventures. Your interviewer does not want to
become a company legend for making a flaming hiring mistake!

Interview-Ending Finesse

If the interviewer's questions move from the past toward the future, the
interview is going well. Make time to ask the following four questions
before the end of the interview. Don't be afraid to speak up—you need
the answers to these questions.

1. Can you offer me this job? (If you want the job, be sure to ask for it;
   20 percent of the people who ask for a job get it.)

2. Do you want me to come back for another interview, perhaps with some
   of the other decision makers here?

3. When may I expect to hear from you?

4. What is the latest I can expect to hear from you?

If it becomes clear that the interviewer doesn't view you as qualified for this
particular job, don't assume all is lost. Be sure to ask these three questions
before you bolt for the door:

1. Do you have questions about my qualifications to do this job? (This gives
   you a chance to make another pitch about your strengths. Make sure your
   response addresses your interviewer's specific concern.)

2. Are there other jobs in your department for which you think I'm qualified?

3. Are there other departments that might hire me?

AFTER AN INTERVIEW

Always send a thank-you note to your interviewer. If more than one person
was involved in the interview, send a thank-you note to each person on the
interview team. (See chapter 4 to review thank-you note basics.)

• Thank each interviewer for his or her time.

• If you enjoyed meeting the interviewer, say so.

• Mention one or two bits of your skills, training, or previous jobs that best
  show your ability to do the job.

Be succinct. A letter of just three or four paragraphs (with three to four sentences in each paragraph) can be read quickly and won't sound like a sales pitch instead of a thank-you. Always make certain your note—whether typed or e-mailed—is grammatically correct, with no spelling errors. Send it within twenty-four hours of your interview.

Here's a thank-you note sample:

(Date)

Dear Mr. Monroe:

Thank you so much for interviewing me for the job of nurse's aide. I was so impressed that you took the time to show me around and introduce me to other employees.

My training makes me very qualified for this job. I hope you agree. My experience helping my grandmother after her last surgery taught me how to work with older patients who are sick or slightly confused.

I hope I'll hear from you on Friday, as you indicated. If not, I'll call you next week.

Sincerely,

Sean Jones

PARACHUTE TIP

Don't overthink writing a thank-you note. Learn a good structure and you can use it over and over. Do an Internet search on "job interview thank-you notes" to find templates.

DON'T GET DISCOURAGED

If your faith in finding your dream job is flagging, ask your contacts to connect you with other young people who have found their dream jobs. Ask these Dream Job Getters to tell you how they did it. Can you adapt what they did to your job search? Find and read inspiring books or articles on people who love their work. Other people's stories can help you stay positive about what is truly possible.

Remember, not many get their dream jobs in their first attempt. It takes lots of steps, lots of hard work. Each time you have a setback, redouble your efforts to find people doing the work you hope to do—the younger in age, the better. If these people encourage you, you probably have the right stuff. If you have the right stuff and work hard to get hired, you will.

REALITY CHECK

After the interview, is your interest in the job as high as when you learned about it? How high is the correlation between your interests and what the employer needs done? If the correlation is low, don't feel bad if you don't get hired. If you aren't enthusiastic about your job, you probably won't be working there long.

YOU'RE HIRED! NOW WHAT?

Congratulations! That hard work paid off and you've been hired. Over the next few weeks, let your contacts and professional network know your job hunt has been successful. Enjoy your good news and be sure to celebrate all your effort.

As you start your new job, is there something else you should be doing? The late John Crystal, author and creative job-search pioneer, once said, "To take charge of your career, you need to look further down the road than headlight range. You need to begin your next job hunt the day you start your current job."

Oof! That's probably not what you wanted to hear right now. But taking charge of your next career move is simply a continuation of what you've already been doing. What's your next step on the way to your true dream job? What training or education will you need? What kind of a work portfolio do you need to build from your current job?

To help you continue on the road to your dream job, we have a few more recommendations for you.

Keep a Job Journal

Each week, spend ten to fifteen minutes making notes about what you did during the week. Is Friday after lunch perfect for updating? Jot down names of projects, tasks, activities, or important meetings. Make notes about what to include in a future job portfolio. Note what you like with a + and use a – for job duties you didn't like. Include committees you've been asked to serve on and the names of professional organizations you've joined. Note any offices you may hold in professional organizations.

Why do this weekly? All new hires think they will never forget the details of their first big job. But in six months, your memory blurs. If you write down all the tasks and responsibilities of your regular job duties and special projects, you won't forget you did them. Your job journal will help with performance reviews and self-evaluations and will put you ahead of the game when you make your next strategic career move in search of your dream job.

Who's in the C-Suite?

As you become familiar with your new work environment, begin to meet and observe people throughout the organization. Who are the up-and-comers? Is there a manager you would rather work for or a division you would rather work in? Get to know the people who have the jobs you want. Get to know their managers, too. Don't say, "I want your job"; you won't build good relations with your colleagues that way. Do ask people about the specifics of their jobs. By doing information interviews at work, you can develop a plan for the next step in your career.

Watch, Listen, and Learn

If you join a business, division, or department that has two or more people, you're entering a situation that has a history. Find out that history. There are ongoing dynamics and power struggles about which you know nothing, yet. As you learn your way around, observe everyone and everything. Don't overdo sharing of personal information or get overly friendly until you know someone's motives. After a few weeks of watching the scene, you'll probably put together what's going on.

Find a Mentor

In fact, find several mentors. If this is a company in which you hope to have a long-term career, find a mentor within the company. If you like the industry, find one or more mentors outside the company. You can pick people who are still working or who have retired. Choose mentors who have achieved the level and kind of success to which you aspire. Meet with your mentors at least twice a year.

We hope that after reading this chapter, you feel more confident about—and maybe even excited about—your first hiring interviews. As with anything else, the more you practice, the more comfortable you'll get—and the closer you'll be to achieving the career of your dreams.

CHAPTER 11

TRENDS AND YOUR CAREER

Your career is under *your* command. Once you are out of school and employed, you can't expect your employer to plan your career advancement for you. Employers aren't much interested in their employees' career development (although most pay attention to their own). Part of managing your career will include being aware of trends that could affect you. *Trend* means "as the issue is currently." Smart young adults keep their futures from being ambushed by keeping track of known or emerging economic, scientific, social, cultural, and global issues that have power to bring change to their lives.

Your job may fit you now, but all jobs are temporary. Keep your parachute up-to-date and your professional network well tuned. You will need both to change jobs quickly. To keep on a career track of *your* choice when the job market is volatile means you have to

• Keep your current job skills sharp.

• Add to them often.

• Qualify for new careers in emerging fields.

PARACHUTE TIP

If you want to keep up with what you need to know to stay employed, spend a few hours at least twice a year finding and reading about workplace trends. Read a top financial or economics periodical or blog at least once a quarter. Read about your field monthly.

TRACKING EMERGING TRENDS

Tracking emerging trends is simply part of your career development. Research keeps you informed. Information helps you create options. Having and knowing options is the best preparation for economic or social change. Early in the career-choice process, knowing the current trends in your favorite fields may affect your pursuit or rejection of a specific career. If you go into a field knowing the changes already under way, you can make plans for how to respond to them. If you do this kind of research repeatedly during your work life, huge changes can't sneak up on you.

In truth, working-age people spend more time filing their nails than managing their careers or researching a strategy to get and keep jobs they like. Recruiters and executive coaches suggest that their clients write a new resume each New Year's Day, whether or not they are job hunting. Although updating your resume at least annually is a good idea, it's not much of a strategy for advancement. Keeping track of new jobs that interest you and trends emerging in your own field is a much better use of your time. Talking with your mentors and colleagues and attending professional functions are efficient ways to track industry changes as well. Some workplace skills are in constant demand. For other skill sets, demand appears to ratchet up overnight. You may find your next career move is into a job that has only just morphed into reality.

Sustainable Careers

The words *sustainable* and *sustainability* may be well known to you. You will certainly hear them more in the coming years. Something *sustainable* means that it can easily be maintained and renewed over time. The term is also used to refer to the use of natural resources without depleting them or destroying the ecology.

What is a sustainable organization or business? To be considered sustainable or green, here are some basic criteria:

• Complies with all environmental regulations

• Conserves energy and water

• Prevents pollution

• Reduces, reuses, and recycles

• Uses renewable energy

• Responsibly measures, controls, and reduces the organization's carbon footprint

DISCOVERY EXERCISE

DISCOVER CAREER TRENDS

What's the top trend in your favorite fields? To discover what challenges you must track, let's pull some information together.

- List any issues you recall being mentioned in your information interviews about where the field is going, what kinds of jobs are emerging, what's being phased out.

- Find and read two or three of the professional journals for your field or industry.

  + What trends are cited?

  + When are they expected to come into play?

  + What are some projections about how this will affect this field or industry?

- Ask your contacts in the field for accurate information about where things are headed.

Do this research for your top three fields or jobs. Are there trends shaping up that might shift your educational goals or make you not want to pursue a job in any one of these fields?

In recent years, the concept of sustainability has permeated our personal and work lives, as well. Sustainability has many implications for your work life. Careers have to be sustainable; otherwise, they can weaken and die. The cost of gaining education after high school, living expenses, any debt for education, and your starting salary all have to be factored into the money side of staying sustainable.

REALITY CHECK

Are you sustainable? To learn the size of your ecological footprint, take the quiz at www.myfootprint.org/en/ visitor_information.

Personal Financial Sustainability

Both a dream job and a good job must be financially sustainable. A job that is financially sustainable covers your bills and those of your dependents, and allows for saving. The definition of *sustainable* given earlier is "something that is easily maintained." If your combined student loan and credit card debt exceeds two-thirds of your starting salary, you won't find it easy to maintain yourself.

As you make decisions about the kind of work you want to do, consider how much the training, internships, or education to qualify for that work will cost you. What would your starting salary be?

If the necessary studies will put you in debt for more than the annual starting salary, that choice is not financially sustainable. This doesn't mean you should permanently give up a career path because it is too expensive to pursue at the moment. You may need to come up with an alternative strategy that will help you achieve short-term and long-term career goals: Pursue other work you enjoy first to build up your education fund. Alternate periods of education or training with work. Get a specialist job in the field for a number of years until you can afford to study exactly what you want. If you research, plan, and follow an effective strategy, you will enjoy your life while you pursue your career dreams.

NOT ALL DEGREES, COURSES OF STUDY, OR MAJORS ARE SUSTAINABLE

In earlier Discovery Exercises, you were asked to list what you don't like as well as what you do. That's because human senses were developed to detect danger. In new situations or locations, if you don't like something or if something doesn't feel right, that's a danger first-alert. Most often, don't-likes move to become preferences rather than indicating dangerous situations.

Since examining the negative is frequently as helpful as looking at the positive, here's a cautionary tale about the consequences of overlooking sustainability at each career-development step.

Your cousin is now living back with her mother. She got her BA in sociology because she wants to help people. It took your cousin seven years to get her degree, a couple of which were spent at a private college from which she dropped out. Your cousin owes more than $53,000. If she had known Liz Weston's two-thirds formula (see page 91), your cousin would have learned that she needed a starting salary of $80,000 to pay her debt and living expenses. Not likely with her degree and major.

Your cousin also doesn't want to leave the area where she went to school. It's a nice-sized college town in a gorgeous setting. Of course, it's saturated with graduates with the same degree as hers, and number crunchers who got BS degrees in sociology and several medical internships and earn three times as much. The hospital does hire BA sociologists, but only those with master's degrees. The starting salaries for master's-level qualifications typically pay less than $50,000 annually.

This was where you stepped in and made your cousin do some research. In a couple of hours of Internet research and a few phone calls, your cousin learned that getting a master's in sociology would cost between $85,000 and $125,000 (or more), depending on the kind of program and the cachet of the master's program. The MA would qualify your cousin for jobs with starting salaries of $42,000 to $53,000.

However, there are hospitals in other parts of the country that do need entry-level sociologists because they are too remote to attract MA sociologists. Several of the hospitals are loan-repayment sites. In exchange for three years of work with pay and benefits, the hospital would repay all her student loans.

Unfortunately, your cousin isn't about to spend the contracted three years in such small towns, even in return for the cancellation of $53,000 in loans immediately and for work she says she would like to do. Pity that.

Job-Market Volatility

Just expect it. Globally, the next decade is not likely to be a calm one. There's just too much political and economic turmoil happening now. How those upheavals will affect financial and job markets in the United States and other countries is unknowable. Best to keep your skills sharp, attend the best training you can afford, and get your side hustle going.

Millennial employment coach Scott Asai defines *side hustle* as turning ideas into income. Scott advises, "The skill set that college should teach, but doesn't, is: How to sell. All your ideas for a side business need to be implemented *now*! If you currently have a job, you can lose it overnight . . . If you're unemployed, it can last a long time. . . . If you're an entrepreneur, you have to keep evolving." (See Scott's blog on side hustle at http://us2.campaign-archive1 .com/?u=fcb8cfe6adf48629ab4478a1c&id=a0104171c7&e=683e6e30ee.)

Your parachute doesn't equate to just one job. The factors you've listed describe attributes of *many* jobs. Your task is to know several that you can move into right away or after a bit of study. At any time in your work life, whether starting out or in the middle, you will always want to know at least three different job goals for which you are well matched. If your current career path abruptly ends, you've got a backup plan: two more ready to pave.

> The long and winding road for the sustainability movement has gone through three distinct phases. The first phase was about information: if we tell everyone what is happening, we'll all make different choices and solve the problem. The second phase was about emotions: if we can connect with our audience on an emotional level, they'll make different choices and solve the problem. The flaw is that we can be deeply moved by the loss of a species or the injustice of a power plant being placed in a poor neighborhood, but that doesn't give us a sense of how to take action in ways that change the systemic condition. The third phase is about self-organization: if we can work together to make sense of our challenges and develop ways to bring our values into action, then our collective, collaborative action can transform our world.
>
> —ALAN BUSH, MA, PROFESSOR OF INDUSTRIAL ECOLOGY AND SUSTAINABLE DESIGN, LENOIR-RHYNE UNIVERSITY

TRENDS TO NOTICE NOW

The very definition of a trend is that it's constantly shifting. Here's what's hot right now: social media jobs, coding, and Massive Open Online Courses (MOOCs for short). We'll also take a look at six emerging megatrend fields of the future.

Social Media Jobs

Social media careers are the new frontier for the field of marketing. It's a marketing tool that has unlimited potential. Social media is used by large corporations and by 87 percent of small businesses as well. People wanting to enter this field should have analytical, communication, and top-level research skills. Also helpful is the ability to think out possible unintended consequences—if you read up on some of the spectacular fails in social media, you realize that this is a job-keeping skill.

Search-engine optimization (SEO) specialist, social media strategist, online community manager, social media marketing manager, and social media marketing coordinator are five social media jobs that have good hiring prospects.

REALITY CHECK

Your best friend, Tibo, wants to take over the sand mine started by his grandfather. Everyone in the family thinks it's a good idea. Tibo took classes in accounting, transportation, contracts, and beginning business law at community college in anticipation of taking over the business. While Tibo was away doing an internship, the city council voted to restrict all large equipment manufacturing to outside the city limits. Tibo's career path changed because public sentiment changed. Economic changes such as new taxes on manufacturing, uncertain energy bills, or a catastrophic accident could have caused this career disruption as well.

Coding

Recruiters and career consultants don't always agree on what makes a good job-search technique. However, on the subject of coding, they now sound like a choir. Both groups recommend that even if you don't envision a life employed in technology, learning to code has multiple advantages—not the least of which is that some young adults who don't think it's for them will fall in love with it.

Many states have programs to help their students learn coding and compete for scholarships. Ask teachers at your school if they can help you find and enroll in these programs. An Internet search will bring up at least a dozen links to different coding sites, both free and for pay. To learn coding in a way that's fun, see www.alice.org.

Massive Open Online Courses (MOOCs)

Massive Open Online Courses were predicted to revolutionize higher education by providing anytime access to high-quality online classes. This prediction hasn't come true just yet, but MOOCs are making waves.

While it's still true that students prefer on-site, in-person learning, as the quality of instructors and video presentations improves, so will student interest in MOOCs. Clearly, MOOCs have an excellent secondary use as well: They can help you decide on a course of study for your higher education. When you know a subject you think you might want to study, take a MOOC. It's one thing to think, "I want to be a neurosurgeon." By checking out a couple of pre-med classes online, you will know before you even apply for college if this choice is going to work for you.

The big deal about MOOCs is that they can seriously reduce what you pay for your degree. Schools that favor on-site learning are not pleased that higher education students now have choices. Just like taking lower-division prerequisites or electives at a community college over the summer adds to your units but costs less in tuition than a university, taking a few MOOCs can lower your overall education costs. This means that the same degree from the same institution could have a widely varying price tag. It's like comparing airfare with a bunch of friends on your ski vacation: No one paid the same for her airfare. Some got incredible deals, and some paid full fare.

Smart higher education consumers will take advantage of MOOCs and be crowing at graduation how they didn't pay retail. William Shatner will be proud.

REALITY CHECK

Although labeled Open and Online, most MOOCs are not free.

Emerging Megatrend Jobs

In the following Expert Advice feature, trend-spotting expert Sharon Jones shares her views on new jobs teens should consider.

EXPERT ADVICE

SIX MEGATRENDS AND FUTURE CAREERS

Sharon Wiatt Jones
www.linkedin.com/in/sharonwiattjones

It's never too soon to start testing out your dreams! High school teachers and college professors are studying global trends to predict the skills needed in the future, since most of the jobs for your generation do not yet exist.

Big Data and High-Performance Computing

Are you good at math and computer science? Learn how to use supercomputers to solve problems, make decisions, and predict trends. Simulate aerodynamics for airplanes and spacecraft; track epidemics and disease outbreaks; identify financial fraud.

Data scientist, statistical analyst, geneticist, quantitative sports analyst

Life Sciences and Medicine

Do you see yourself making an impact in health care? Personalized medicine will include prescription drugs and chemotherapy with less risk of side effects. Advanced technologies such as prosthetic devices, adaptive equipment for people with disabilities, and organ transplants are transforming the future.

Diagnostic medical sonographer, cardiovascular technologist, informatics nurse specialist, biomedical engineer, bioinformatics scientist

Energy and the Environment

Are you concerned about the environment? You could choose a career to help improve the cleanliness of air, land, water, or the food supply.

Environmental engineer, sustainability specialist, environmental economist, industrial ecologist, brownfield redevelopment specialist

Advanced Manufacturing and Nanomaterials

Do you have an insatiable curiosity about how things work? Nano-materials are used in industries such as medicine and health (pros-thetics, dental implants), transportation (spacecraft, driverless cars), and consumer goods (mobile phones, wearable fitness devices). These materials can be thin and lightweight, with special character-istics such as heat resistance, fluorescence, strength, or flexibility.

Mechatronics engineer, nanotechnology engineering technician, photonics engineer, solar energy systems engineer, additive manufacturing engineer

Online Education and Entertainment

Online education has made university education and skills training much more accessible. Medical students can use computer simula-tions to perform virtual autopsies, and some autistic children learn to speak by playing "serious games."

Game designer/developer, computer interface designer, instructional technologist, animation artist

Globalization

As residents in former emerging economies (Brazil, Russia, India, and China) and new markets (Indonesia, Malaysia, the Philippines, South Africa, Thailand, Turkey, and Vietnam) become more pros-perous, they will be able to afford more health care services and consumer goods.

Computational linguist, voice developer, speech output designer, social localization specialist

For further information on trends, read *Abundance: The Future Is Better Than You Think* by Peter H. Diamandis and Steven Kotler.

CHAPTER 12

BEYOND YOUR DREAM JOB
create the life you want

You've heard the saying "There's more to life than work." We agree whole-heartedly, and would add that there's even more to life than the very good and fulfilling work that we want you to find in your dream job. While our main focus is to prepare you to find that dream job, we do have a deeper purpose for writing this book: to help you get the whole life you want.

In this chapter, we invite you to explore what that whole life means for you. We'll ask you to reflect on the people, things, and activities that you want to include in your life. Next, we'll ask you to delve a bit deeper and consider the underpinnings of your life, your values and beliefs, and your "philosophy of life." After that, we want you to look at the people you respect and admire—your role models—and consider how they can help you become the person you want to be. Lastly, we'll invite you to look at your purpose or mission in life. What were you put on earth to do? For each of these areas, we'll ask you to spend time reflecting on different aspects of your life—how you want to live and what type of person you want to be. Although you can learn from how other people answer these questions, to get the life you want, you must know the answers for yourself.

ENVISION YOUR LIFE, DESIGN YOUR FUTURE

Reading and doing the Discovery Exercises, you've spent time discovering what you want in your dream job. But what else do you want? How do you want to fill hours outside of work? What about being alive is most important to you? What kind of life do you want? Knowing what you want is the first step to making that life happen. Don't expect these ideas to just pop into your head; it will take focused thought. Do you want your life to include . . .

• Friends, family, a life partner, children, pets?

• Sports and outdoor activities?

• Cultural activities (theater, music, dance)?

• Travel and time for hobbies?

• Involvement with community or religious organizations?

• Participation in political or environmental causes?

There are many more things you can do with your time outside work. This short list is to get you thinking what you want in your life—what you enjoy doing now and want to continue doing. Is anything missing from your life that you want in your future? What matters is that you become aware of how you want to spend your time. That way, you'll be sure to carve out enough time to enjoy the activities that make you happy.

What kind of family life do you want to have as an adult, particularly in relation to your work? Will it be like the family life you have now, or will it be different? Kyle, age fifteen, wants something different because, as he puts it, "My dad hides out at work." Family life often gets neglected these days. Parents now spend 40 percent less time with their children than they did in the 1960s. If you want to have children, what kind of parent do you want to be? What kind of relationships with your children do you want to have?

The following exercise will help you envision your future and the way you want to live your life, including what and whom you want to play a part in it.

> Do what you feel in your heart to be right—
> for you'll be criticized anyway. . . . In the
> long run, we shape our lives, and we shape
> ourselves. The process never ends until we die.
> And the choices we make are ultimately
> our own responsibility.
> —ELEANOR ROOSEVELT, DIPLOMAT AND ACTIVIST

DISCOVERY EXERCISE

PICTURE YOUR IDEAL LIFE

Pretend a magic wand has been waved over your life, giving you everything that's important to you. Have fun with this, but give yourself plenty of time to think about what matters most. It may take days or a few weeks complete this exercise. Let what's really important to you rise to the surface. The goal is to have a visual image of your ideal life. Once you are satisfied with the picture you create, hang it up where you can see it. As other ideas for the life you want arise, add them to your Ideal Life Picture. You'll need the following materials for this exercise. Use your computer graphic-art skills, too.

- A large piece of white paper
- Colored pencils or pens
- Old magazines that you can cut up
- Scissors
- Glue

Draw pictures or symbols, or create a collage to express visually the kind of life you want to live. The following questions will get you thinking about what you want to include in your picture. Don't limit yourself to ideas from the list; add whatever is important to you.

- In your ideal life, where do you live (city, suburb, rural area, on an island, in the mountains)?
- What kind of house or living space do you want?
- What is your neighborhood like?
- Who is with you (friends, family, pets)?
- Where do you work? What do you do for a living?
- Do you travel? Where do you want to go? Where do you vacation?
- What activities—sports, cultural, religious/spiritual, family, community—do you participate in?

Work on your picture until you feel it truly represents the life you want. Now, look at your picture again. What do you need to do to help make this ideal life happen? Because you can't do everything at once, choose one area that you can affect now. Return to chapter 7 to review how to set short-term and long-term goals. Having a picture of what you want your life to be is an important step to make it your reality.

Once you have a concrete vision of your future, let's explore more deeply how you want to live that life and who you want to be. This includes discovering the unique contribution you have to make to the world and finding meaning in your life and in the world around you. As you live, love, and learn more about life, you'll create—spoken or unspoken—a philosophy of life, a way in which you understand and view life events and people.

A philosophy of life helps you to interpret and understand your life experiences. A philosophy of life also assists you in making decisions. Know what is important to you? Your beliefs will be reflected in your decisions. For some, the meaning of life may be grounded in religious or spiritual beliefs and the interaction of those beliefs with life experiences; for others, it will grow more directly out of their life experiences. We invite you to take twenty minutes now to think about your philosophy of life. Completing the exercise will take a bit longer. This exercise isn't a one-off; try to come back to it every couple of years. You'll notice that some of your values are constant, and some change.

Your philosophy of life shapes everything that you do, as well as everything you are and are becoming. It shapes all aspects of your life, whether or not you are aware of it doing so. Just as you created a concrete vision of your future life in the preceding Discovery Exercise, writing out your philosophy of life will help you recognize the values by which you want to live your life. Knowing what you want is the first step to making it happen.

> The goal of life is to make your heartbeat match the beat of the universe, to match your nature with Nature.
>
> —JOSEPH CAMPBELL, MYTHOLOGIST AND AUTHOR

DISCOVERY EXERCISE

WRITING YOUR PHILOSOPHY OF LIFE

Everyone needs an "operating manual" for his or her life. That's what a philosophy of life is. It identifies what you value most in life and articulates how those values guide your decisions.

Begin by writing down what is most important to you (family, friends, money, art, freedom, chocolate-chip cookies, or whatever). Why are these important to you? Why do you want them to be a part of your life? This exercise overlaps with the previous exercise—friends and family may come up in both exercises, for example. That's fine. Now, go a bit further and think about particular qualities that are important to you, such as truth, integrity, peace, compassion, or forgiveness.

Next, list the beliefs by which you intend to live your life (for example, all people are created equal, creation is sacred, or love is more powerful than hate). How will you face difficult times in your life? How do you hope you'll react to obstacles that may block your goals? How will you deal with loss, frustration, or death?

Take time to think about what you value and believe. Think about what makes your life meaningful. Work on your philosophy of life for ten minutes a day for a week, or spend some time on it each weekend for a month or two. What emerges as you reflect on these important matters? Your philosophy of life will evolve and grow as you do. Revisit and revise your philosophy of life from time to time.

If you're ever disappointed with yourself or your life, ask yourself these questions:

• Am I paying attention to what I value most?

• Am I living my life by what I most deeply believe?

If you hit a rough patch in life, reviewing your philosophy of life will help you assess what went wrong and give you ideas to get back on track.

BECOME THE PERSON YOU WANT TO BE

As you picture your ideal life and articulate your philosophy of life, you may also want to reflect on what kind of person you want to be. Lisa, age fifteen, wants to be an adult who doesn't spend all her life at work. "Sometimes adults make it seem like all they do is work. That doesn't make being an adult very attractive." What makes being an adult attractive to you?

When you think about the person you want to be, you'll undoubtedly think about people who are important to you—people who have helped, inspired, befriended, or supported you through tough times. Who are the people you respect and admire? Who are your role models? Reflect on those people who, by their lives and example, can help you become the person you want to be.

Reflecting on the traits you value—those that you most admire in other people—can help you cultivate those traits in yourself. Arrange to talk with one or more of your role models about a trait of theirs that you particularly admire: their compassion, intellect, wit, honesty, or ability to make people feel comfortable. Ask them how they developed that trait. Who are their role models? Do they have suggestions to help you develop that trait in your own life?

> Those who preserve their integrity remain unshaken by the storms of daily life. They do not stir like leaves on a tree or follow the herd where it runs. In their mind remains the ideal attitude and conduct of living. This is not something given to them by others. It is their roots. . . . It is a strength that exists deep within them.
>
> **—ANONYMOUS**

MY ROLE MODELS

Take a sheet of paper and turn it so that the long edge is horizontal. Fold the sheet in half, crease it, and then fold it in half again. You should have four columns of equal width.

Title the first column "Names of people I admire." Under that heading, make a list of people you admire. These can be real people you know or have known, historical figures, or fictional characters from books, movies, comic books, or TV.

Title the second column "What I admire about them." Think about each person in the first column, then write down what you admire about them.

Title the third column "Do I have this trait?" Read over the traits you've written for each of the people you admire. Ask yourself, "Do I have this trait? Do I want to have this trait?" Write your answers in the third column.

Label the last column "How can I develop this trait?" Answer this question for each trait or attribute you'd like to develop or strengthen.

DISCOVER YOUR LIFE PURPOSE OR CALLING

Ever heard someone say, "I don't consider what I do *work*; it's my calling"? Adults, young or otherwise, want to feel that they are honoring their own talents and doing work that is more than earning money, more than even a dream job. Some people feel they were put on earth to do something, or to do particular things. For those who believe this way, finding their calling can become a mission.

Is a sense of purpose or calling important to you? Reading this book, reflecting on how you want to live your life, what you most deeply value and believe, and whom you most deeply admire will help you uncover your unique purpose for being here on earth. Your reflections on these questions, along with the other explorations you've made in this book, will help you find your purpose or calling—that is, what you are alive to do.

Perhaps you will be helped by this definition. American theologian Frederick Buechner defines vocation as the "place where your deep gladness meets the world's deep need." You need look no further for your calling or mission in life than what makes you deeply happy. Once you know that, choose whichever of the many needs of this world calls most loudly to you.

Whether you seek a calling or work you enjoy, always remember that you have gifts to offer the world. The gift you are and the gifts you offer are unique. Only you can be you. What unique gift of yours can make the world a better place?

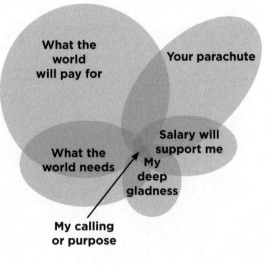

THE POWER OF VISION

Successful people believe in the power of vision. They craft visions of what they want to create or make happen, and they apply these ideas to their personal and commercial lives.

So here's your chance to be a video director. If you were to create a video of your life, from now through achieving your dreams or even your death, what would it be like?

Would your story be a romantic comedy? Drama? Sitcom? Stand-up routine? Musical? Docudrama or MTV? How would you organize episodes about your ages, ah-ha moments, or hard-won wisdom? How would you show your future? (No tragedies—to prevent your life from becoming a tragedy, you think things out before you act them out.)

Write a script for your story. Start with yourself from eighteen onward.

- What happens in your life as you age?

- Who do you work for (yourself or an employer)? Who do you work with? Where do you work? Where do you live?

- What do you do at work? What do you do with your free time?

- What brings the most joy to your life?

- What obstacles do you encounter? How do you overcome them?

- Block out the scenes. Add director's notes for who does what in each scene.

- Work and rework your script until you feel it's ready to be enacted.

- Who will you get to play the different characters?

Roll cameras!

> My mission in life is not merely to survive, but to thrive; and to do so with some passion, some compassion, some humor, and some style.
> —MAYA ANGELOU, POET

> Don't confuse life and work. It is much easier
> to write a resume than to craft a spirit.
> —ANNA QUINDLEN, WRITER

OUR WISH FOR YOU

In closing, we wish you well as you discover yourself, design your future, and live out your mission in life. Finding the job you want and creating the life you want can be done only by you. May you find work that challenges, satisfies, and delights. May that work be part of a whole life that is good and fulfilling in every way. May you live out your life purpose—your mission—and share your unique gifts to make the world a better place.

As you move from teen to adult, we hope you will: Tell the truth. Stand up for those who can't speak for themselves. Take some (manageable) risks. Be a bit cautious. Be thorough. Be persistent. Be kind. Prepare to deal with the good and the disappointing parts of life. Live fully, love deeply, and always remember that decision by decision, day by day, you create your life and your future. The adventure of your life is waiting. Go meet it.

ABOUT THE AUTHORS

Carol Christen is a career strategist who has worked extensively with teenagers and young adults since she was one herself. Carol lives in Butte, Montana, where her daughter is a family practice physician. She and her husband live at the eastern foot of the Rocky Mountains. Neighbors are moose, elk, deer, antelope, cottontails, chipmunks, and dozens of bird species. Contact Carol or learn more about her work through:

www.Parachute4Teens.com
Twitter: parachute4teens
Facebook: facebook.com/parachute4teens
LinkedIn: www.linkedin.com/in/carolchristencareerconsultant

Richard N. Bolles has been a leader in the career development field for more than forty years and is the author of *What Color Is Your Parachute?* He lives in the San Francisco Bay Area.

INDEX

N

Network building
  benefits of, 46, 47–48
  definition of, 44
  goal of, 46
  informal vs. formal, 46–47
  social media and, 117–19
  See also Contacts; Information
    interviews

O

Organizations
  researching, 141–42
  small, 146
  targeting, 142, 146

P

Parachute diagram. *See* My
    Parachute diagram
Part-time work, 65–66, 82–83
Party exercise, 27–29, 31
Passion, finding, 22–23
Peace Corps, 83
People
  favorite types of, 26–30, 31, 33
  skills with, 10, 17
Physical skills, 10, 15
Prioritizing, 20, 105
Professionalism, 112, 113

R

References, 146
Remedial classes, 80
Responsibility, level of, 38, 41
Resumes, 115–16, 146–47
Role models, 176–77

S

Salary
  ideal, 38–39, 41
  information on, 39
  job satisfaction and, 94–95
  of recent college graduates, 90
  researching, 89
Self-Directed Search (SDS), 29
Skills
  best, 9, 18, 20
  can-do vs. want-to, 18
  definition of, 9, 10
  desired by employers, 95–96
  enjoyable, 9
  essential, 65, 74
  identifying, 11–14, 18–21

interests and, 9
  interpersonal (with people), 10, 17
  job-search, 67–69
  knowledge (work content), 20–21
  mental (with information), 10, 16
  physical (with things), 10, 15
  self-management (personal traits),
    19, 21–22
  teamwork, 96
  transferable (functional), 10, 12,
    18–19, 20
Skill TIPs, 10, 13, 15–17, 18
Social entrepreneurs, 58
Social media
  as career-planning tool, 116–19,
    125–27
  characteristics of, 109
  jobs in, 167
  popular sites, 111
  possibilities of, 109–10
  safety and, 124–25
State Civilian Conservation Corps, 83
Student loans, 88–92
Summer work, 65–66
Sustainability, 162, 164–65, 166

T

Teamwork skills, 96
Telephone calls, 143, 146
Thank-you notes, 54–56, 139, 156–57
To-do lists, 106–7
Traits, personal, 19, 21–22
Twitter, 111, 116, 120, 123, 124

U

University Pages, 122

V

Vacancies, 145
Vision, power of, 179
Visual resumes, 115–16
Voice mail, 143

W

Web
  creating a presence on, 112–13,
    114–15, 126, 127
  privacy and, 126
  resumes on, 115–16
  See also Social media
Work environment, ideal, 34–38
Work ethic, 96
Work permits, 62